IN TH
A F

IN THE EYES OF
A RASIKA

a connoisseur's views on
art and politics, art and science

Juliet Reynolds

BLUEJAY BOOKS

An imprint of Srishti Publishers & Distributors
New Delhi & Calcutta

BLUEJAY BOOKS
An imprint of SRISHTI PUBLISHERS & DISTRIBUTORS
64-A, Adhchini
Sri Aurobindo Marg
New Delhi 110 017

First published by *BLUEJAY BOOKS* in 2003

©Juliet Reynolds 2003

ISBN 81-88575-12-7
Rs. 295

Cover & Book design by
Creative Concept
40/223, C.R. Park
New Delhi 110 019

To Geraldine, my mother
and
to Anil
who made me

Acknowledgements

I wish to thank the following for their contributions to this book: my editor and friend, Partha Chatterjee, whose expert knowledge and sound advice kept my restless mind focussed; my friends and neighbours, Rita Chakravarti, Roma Mazumdar, Sumanta and Bizeth Banerjee, Ghayur and Patricia Alam, whose moral support and keen interest in my work gave me much needed encouragement during the writing; my cousin, David Mahon who encouraged me from afar; my staff, Balbir, Swamy and Tilka who tended to my needs and bore my tantrums; my autistic foster son, Neema, my lively menagerie and my plants who kept me cheerful and rooted to the ground.

Acknowledgement is also due to Jenny Naipaul, former Arts Editor of *The Spectator*, and Vinod Mehta, former Editor of *The Pioneer*. Thanks to their interest in my work, these publications carried many of my articles and opinion pieces during the late 1980s and early 90's. Some of the passages in this book are drawn from these writings.

Introduction

In *The Eyes of a Rasika*, as the subtitle suggests, is a book that opens up views on art and its relationship with politics and science. And in writing it I have attempted, as far as possible, to make this complex subject accessible to the layperson. In an age like ours, when most people lead busy, stressful lives, the average reader has little time to spare on issues affecting her or him indirectly or imperceptibly. Hence the book is intended to be 'user friendly', to employ a term much favoured in modern parlance. Hopefully, it can be picked up and read at any section without necessarily having followed the whole argument. At the same time, the issues it addresses will be clearer if the reader takes time to look at them in entirety.

I make no pretence of having covered every aspect of these issues. Rather, it has been my intention to raise questions on art that in the main are neglected, especially in India. For far too long, art has been obfuscated by its practitioners, experts and those who control its promotion. This is a pattern that needs to be broken. The layperson has a right to know why so much fuss is made about art and artists, a right to have a say in art's projection. Equally, she or he has a right to know that the mystification of art both historic and contemporary is a political issue that can only be rectified or challenged by a scientific approach to the subject.

But if the layperson has such rights, the question to be asked is why she or he should demand them. What is so compelling about art that the layperson needs to understand it in an unjust world torn apart by wars, conflicts, fanaticism, and intolerable economic and social disparities? Part of the answer has already been suggested. Because art has a political face, it joins up with the broader reality of our lives. It affords a microcosmic view of the macrocosm - our unjust world. So to have knowledge of it is to better understand our times and our societies.

Yet art serves this end not only on account of its political face. When it is good it also offers aesthetic experience, and this should never be underplayed. One of the great aims of art is to make people more sensitive to their own and others' reality. To cultivate the capacity for aesthetic appreciation - to become a connoisseur or *rasika* - is to work towards the discovery of the whole human being. But, again, this cannot be achieved without placing art in the light of science.

A great deal of this book is devoted to the science of aesthetics, with special emphasis on *rasa*, the brilliant aesthetic system contributed to the world by India. This is a subject that leads into fascinating areas of human knowledge and experience, relevant to all world cultures and ages. Similarly, I have explored art and politics in a universal and historic context, with a view to understanding contemporary Indian reality. In both essays there is a marked emphasis on the sorry state of contemporary Indian art and its world. And if my words sometimes ring harshly this is because it is my heartfelt desire to see a renewal of the spirit and energies - human and creative - that once prevailed in this country.

I have called myself a *rasika* or connoisseur with a modicum of trepidation since I claim a very limited understanding of many of India's traditions, particularly the literary. However, despite the many references I make to the arts in general, including film, this is essentially a book about visual art. And in this domain, particularly with respect to Indian tradition, I can claim a capacity for deep appreciation. Indeed, it is through my explorations of Indian classical art that I have acquired not only greater connoisseurship of western art but also a better understanding of contemporary art and its shortcomings.

Since the writing is focused on art related issues, it does not call for the glossy colour plates that normally accompany texts on art. The illustrations have been selected to throw light on the arguments, but they are by no means comprehensive. In some cases, the artists discussed are not visually represented because colour is the key to understanding their expression. Readers who find this a shortcoming can only be urged to make their own explorations in libraries or via the Internet. As already stated, this book is meant to inspire a process of thinking, and it is hopeful that the curious reader will fulfill this aim through images as much as words.

Juliet Reynolds
New Delhi
March, 2003

PART I

ART AND POLITICS

Art and politics: the very mention of the two in the same breath is enough to raise eyebrows in the course of most conversations. Even art specialists or laypeople with a fair understanding of art tend to assume that if the two spheres do indeed meet, this is at the level of art politics, a matter of little consequence to the public. Art politics is petty in nature and is mainly concerned with the clash of interests between established artists or artists who aspire to join the establishment. The politics of art has much larger implications.

Contrary to the expectations perhaps raised by the term, the politics of art does not merely embrace art with a direct political content, which in the main is sheer propaganda. Rather, it means that one side of all art is political in character because it is always produced within a politically determined society. Moreover, art always serves the interests of its patrons, generally the ruling elite, which gives it a political purpose.

In recent years, incidents have occurred in India and neighbouring countries to make people aware that art can have political fallout. The attack on M.F. Husain by Hindu fanatics for his depiction of nude goddesses is a case in point. Another is the destruction of Afghanistan's Buddhist heritage by the Taliban regime.

But the politics of art is still not explained by incidents of this kind. Nor is it fully explained by the colossal politicisation of art that has occurred over the past century under totalitarian regimes. This is, however, a hugely important point and some light is thrown on it by the passages reproduced on pages 14 to 17. It may be noted that the tone of Hitler's speech on 'degenerate art' is echoed with even greater virulence in the speech delivered in the US Congress during the witch-hunt era. This was the era when American communists and their sympathisers, real and imaginary, were hounded by the State for alleged subversive activities.

André Breton and Leon Trotsky's critique of Nazi and Stalinist art policy provides a necessary counterpoint to both speeches, but in its opening lines it echoes our own times rather too closely for comfort. The passage from a speech by the English sculptor, Henry Moore takes an altogether different line. But it nonetheless highlights some very important points about the situation of the artist under changing politico-economic circumstances.

With respect to the place of art in politics, a vital observation is made by the essayist, Walter Benjamin. A German Jew, Benjamin was tragically compelled to commit suicide in 1940 in order to escape Nazi capture. But in the preceding years he had become acutely aware that Hitler's huge ability to mesmerise the masses owed a great deal to his exploitation of art, particularly film. In *The Work of Art in the Age of Mechanical Reproduction* he asserts:

> The logical result of Fascism is the introduction of aesthetics into political life....
> All efforts to render politics aesthetic culminate in one thing: war.

Benjamin's words are of the utmost contemporary relevance. With television as the medium, the aesthetic of war is a part of people's daily lives across the world. Into our homes come nuclear explosions of breathtaking splendour, armoured caravans crossing deserts reminiscent of scenes from Lawrence of Arabia, sleek warplanes in geometric formation, shining weapons of mass destruction designed like props in science fiction films, serried rows of troops aligned for inspection like automatons. Benjamin explains the logic behind the aesthetic:

The horrible features of imperialistic warfare are attributable to the discrepancy between the tremendous means of production and their inadequate utilization in the process of production - in other words, to unemployment and the lack of markets . . . Mankind, which in Homer's time was an object of contemplation for the Olympian gods, now is one for itself. Its self-alienation has reached such a degree that it can experience its own destruction as aesthetic pleasure of the first order.

When one considers that Benjamin wrote this close to seventy years ago, one has to admit with reluctance to the truth of the saying, 'the more things change, the more they are the same'.

Coming back to the main argument, if politics means the way a society is organised and ruled, then it follows that anything which is a tool towards that end is political in nature. In this sense, art has been political for tens of thousands of years: in the Old Stone Age, images were created on the walls of caves or rock shelters because they helped to ensure the success of a hunt. And in all subsequent epochs, art has served organisational purposes of different kinds, bringing it into direct or indirect relationship with politics.

Before proceeding to examine this relationship further, one should heed a note of caution sounded by Peter Selz in *Theories of Modern Art*. As he underlines:

The relationship between art and politics within the total cultural framework is extremely complex and cannot be defined in those simplified Marxist terms which would explain both art and politics as symptoms of a basic economic substructure. The patriotic subject matter and hard heroic form of David's

Neoclassicism, for example, was a cause as well as an effect of the French Revolution of which David himself was one of the decisive leaders... nobody has been more aware of the impact of ideas including works of art on the economic-political condition than the leaders of totalitarian states.

Selz is right about the simplified Marxist approach to the subject because this ignores the mutuality of the relationship. Here the example of Jacques-Louis David is most appropriate. The success of David's paintings as direct political propaganda is probably unsurpassed in the history of world art. For instance, one of his works, *The Oath of the Horatii*, an allegorical call to arms, created waves in Italy as much as in France. When it was exhibited in David's studio in Rome in 1785, the crowds strewed in front of it a carpet of flowers. And when it was transported back to France amidst official opposition, its impact on the public was portentous. In *The Romantic Rebellion*, Kenneth Clark notes that when the painting was on view in Paris

> it created an effect of which those of us who remember the first appearance of Picasso's Guernica may be able to form some conception. Suddenly, through a work of art, men became conscious of moral responsibility.

Guernica by Pablo Picasso is discussed later on. For now it only needs to be remembered that this work is generally regarded as the most political painting of the 20th century. However, unlike David's work, it had no direct influence on political events.

The fact that art can directly influence politics does not mean, as Selz seems to believe, that the economic substructure can be ignored. Economics at base refers to modes of survival and production and to the relationship between producers and consumers. To suggest that either art or politics is independent of these factors would be as preposterous as to agree that man lives by bread alone.

In *The Philosophy of Art History*, Arnold Hauser presents a lucid historical overview of this complex subject. This is how he begins:

> Culture serves to protect society. Spiritual creations, traditions, conventions, and institutions are but ways and means of social organization. Religion, philosophy, science and art all have their place in the struggle to preserve society. To confine oneself to art, it is first of all a tool of magic, a means of ensuring the livelihood of the primitive horde of hunters. Then it becomes an instrument of animistic religion, used to influence good and bad spirits in the interest of the community. Gradually this is transformed into a magnification of the almighty gods and their earthly representatives, by hymn and panegyric, through statues of gods and kings. Finally, in the form of more or less open propaganda, it is employed in the interests of a close group, a clique, a political party or social class...

Art as a tool of magic and of animistic religion is discussed further on, making it possible to take a leap in time to the beginnings of recorded history and look at the magnification of gods and kings. Among the earliest civilisations, we can find the most apt examples in the monumental statues of the Egyptian pharaohs, commissioned and raised all over their territories as a perpetual reminder of their divine authority and of the insignificance of the people. Later, the Greek and Roman rulers would proclaim their glory through temples like the Parthenon and the Pantheon, great sculpted deities and portrait statues, triumphal arches and columns.

And so it was in India. The pillars of Ashoka, crowned with sculptures, carrying his message of peace and reconciliation are a more obvious example of the propagandistic value of art. But the same truth applies to all the great monuments of ancient India, from the *stupas* at Barhut and Sanchi to the temples at Ellora. While the narrative art of the *stupas* projected the Buddha's humanitarian philosophy, the temples were commissioned to magnify the name of the great god, Shiva and the ruling patron dynasties. Clearly they fulfilled this with great effect.

In *Representing the Body: gender issues in Indian art*, Vidya Dehejia offers an explanation of the way art then worked as propaganda:

> ...before the age of mechanical reproduction of visual images... paintings occupied an influential position of great power. We should not underestimate the authority and inspiration provided to its viewers by ancient imagery. Art is a form of rhetoric, a deliberate, contrived and regulated means of persuasion. We tend to think of rhetoric as a verbal skill; the importance of visual forms of rhetoric is only just beginning to be appreciated. Its power of persuasion, often insidious as against the more direct verbal rhetoric, should not be underestimated.

In the European Renaissance, which saw the revival of many of the traditions of ancient Rome, the most striking example of a sacred artwork of propagandistic intent was the ceiling and altar mural painted by Michelangelo in the Sistine Chapel. Situated at the heart of the Vatican City, the work was commissioned by Pope Julius II, a highly ambitious patron who foresaw the possibilities of great name for himself and his Church. In one sense he turned out to be right: no sacred artwork since has surpassed

Michelangelo's in scale, impact or fame. But Julius was wrong in that the greatest share of the glory would, in the long term, belong to the artist.

The Church of Rome, which held political sway over much of Europe even in the wake of the Protestant reform movements, reaped incalculable benefits from its patronage of art. Yet there is a strong case for arguing that the role of art in organising society was even greater in India than in Europe. The art of the Buddhist sanctuaries and Hindu temples was no different from Christian art in that it was designed to propagate an ideology, a system of faith. But while Christian art was a magnificent celebration of suffering, martyrdom and death, the Buddhists and Hindus brought adherents into their fold through sensuous, tactile imagery that celebrated life. This must have made it all the more attractive.

Richard Lannoy agrees that Indian visual imagery has always had a special kind of power. In *The Speaking Tree* he says:

> India's is a sensuous culture, and the new configurations mapped out through the plastic arts have always had a powerful, formative influence on the quality of life. Order, balance, and rhythmic sequence have a much more direct and important role to play in the creation of a culture than is generally supposed. They are the tools, to be precise, with which to *make* order, reveal connections.

Today, in a negative sense, Bollywood films have taken over this role. Despite or because of their inanity, they are highly seductive, and they hold society together like no other form of cultural expression. But by making people all the more unthinking, all the more compliant, they help the ruling classes maintain the status quo. Lalitha Gopalan highlights this point in her essay *Coitus Interruptus and Love Story in Indian Cinema*. She argues that the love story, which is

9

central to popular films, not only upholds patriarchal and feudal values, but also serves narrow nationalist interests. As she asserts:

> Indian cinematic materiality, especially editing, is shaped and structured by a tight relationship between the state and the film industry. Contradictions between the state's interests in the formation of national taste through censorship regulations and the film industry's interests in spectatorial pleasure are most aggressively played out through images of the female body on screen. At the same time the film industry...is a willing accomplice in the production of naturalised national subjects and spaces.

Obviously, the films Gopalan discusses are a far cry from art, if we take it that art is a creative activity demanding imagination and originality as much as skill. However, as propaganda, such films are matchless. One can truly call them the opium of the masses. Art is never an opiate. It can be a balm to soothe the soul, but it never desensitises. To the contrary, one of its main roles is to make people more sensitive, to make them question things as they are.

Art's complete removal from the masses came about when patronage passed from the hands of religious hierarchies and monarchies into those of the bourgeoisie. To be more precise, the new patrons emanated from 'the grand bourgeoisie', the capitalist class grown rich on colonial exploitation and on the vast profits reaped from the Industrial Revolution. As the owners and managers of industries, members of this class saw themselves as distinct from the shopkeepers and clerks with whom they shared the same bourgeois origins. Art patronage was one of the chief ways through which they could demonstrate their superiority over 'the petty bourgeoisie' and their equality with the aristocracy and landed gentry.

With this development, the value of art as propaganda became closely linked to its monetary value. Although the transition took place gradually, by around the mid-19th century, paintings had become luxurious commodities to be invested in and traded like stocks and shares or gold.

It was precisely in reaction to the commodification of artworks that a new philosophy of art arose. This was 'art for art's sake' whose chief proponent was the French poet and art critic, Charles Baudelaire. 'Art for art's sake' struck at the heart of bourgeois hypocrisy. Here was a class of patrons who, on the one hand, purported to be paragons of cultivation and refinement and, on the other, saw art as a means of accumulating greater and greater wealth.

As noted by the Austrian poet and critic, Ernst Fischer, Baudelaire's poetry was designed to shock the sensibilities of the smug bourgeoisie. In *The Necessity of Art*, Fischer says:

> For the vulgar hypocrite and the anaemic aesthete, beauty is an escape from reality, a cloying holy picture, a cheap sedative: but the beauty which rises out of Baudelaire's poetry is…like the angel of wrath holding the flaming sword… Dressed up poverty, hidden disease, and secret vice lie revealed before its radiant nakedness. It is as though capitalist civilization had been brought before a kind of revolutionary tribunal…

Ironically, however, 'art for art's sake' soon came to suit bourgeois patrons by providing them with an ideological justification - a way of demonstrating higher motives - for acquiring art. The patron could now claim that he was sponsoring an activity that was not utilitarian and vulgar like the manufacture of goods. This is why Hauser strongly refutes the popular notion that 'art for art's sake' is apolitical. As he says on the subject of this philosophy:

> ...it performs an important social function by providing men with a means of expressing their power and their "conspicuous leisure". Indeed, it achieves much more than that, promoting the interests of a certain social stratum by the mere portrayal and implicit acknowledgement of its moral and aesthetic standards of value.

Under this new form of patronage, the true artist faced a tragic dilemma. Walter Benjamin sums this up in his analysis of the motivations of Baudelaire. About the poet he states:

> He was the first to realise and this realisation had immense consequences that the bourgeoisie was in the process of withdrawing its commission from the artist.

This may appear to contradict the previous statement on the rise of bourgeois patronage, but what Benjamin means is the bourgeoisie's throwing the artist into the arms of free enterprise. In ancient and feudal times and in the early capitalist age, he could at least depend on the ruling class for steady sustenance. Now his survival was no longer guaranteed. Benjamin goes on to ask what the withdrawal entailed.

> What steady commission could take its place? No class was likely to supply it; the likeliest place from which a living could be earned was the investment market... But the nature of the market...was such that it imposed a manner of production, as well as a way of life, very

different from those of earlier poets. Baudelaire was obliged to claim a poet's dignity in a society which had no more dignity of any kind to give away.

In many ways, this reflects the position of the artist in contemporary India. Since art patrons constitute a miniscule elite, they can only sustain a small minority of the country's artists. Therefore, those artists who are unable to be part of this minority, because they are either powerless or unwilling to conform, are thrown into the uncertain arms of fate to seek a livelihood. The sensitive artist with genuine gifts will find it hardest to claim dignity in this alienating situation.

And why only the artist? The same can be said of most of the urban work force, the lower income middle-class included. Under the form of society in question, the true artist shares the fate of his people and this inevitably reflects in his work. This is not the same thing as slogan mongering, forcing a political or social message into his art to prove his commitment to the world. The artist's feelings of social alienation and vulnerability are deeply personal. But he can communicate these feelings through his art because the majority of his fellow human beings also experience them without being able to express them. They can, therefore, recognise themselves and their feelings in the artist's work.

Cubism, Dadaism, Futurism, Impressionism, etc. have nothing to do with our German people. For these concepts are neither old nor modern, but are only the artifactitious stammerings of men to whom God has denied the grace of a truly artistic talent...

I have observed among the pictures submitted here, quite a few paintings which make one actually come to the conclusion that the eye shows things differently to certain human beings than the way they really are, that is, that there really are men who see the present population of our nation only as rotten cretins; who, on principle, see meadows blue, skies green, clouds sulphur yellow, and so on, or, as they say, experience them as such...

Either these so-called "artists" really see things this way and therefore believe in what they depict; then we would have to examine their eyesight-deformation to see if it is the product of a mechanical failure or of inheritance. In the first case, these unfortunates can only be pitied; in the second case, they would be the object of great interest to the Ministry of Interior of the Reich which would then have to take up the question of whether further inheritance of such gruesome malfunctioning of the eyes cannot at least be checked. If, on the other hand, they themselves do not believe in the reality of such impressions but try to harass the nation with this humbug for other reasons, then such an attempt falls within the jurisdiction of the penal law.

ADOLF HITLER

from his speech at the opening of the exhibition
'Degenerate Art', 1937

*M*r. Speaker, quite a few individuals in art, who are sincere in purpose, honest in intent, but with only a superficial knowledge of the complicated influences that surge in the art world of today, have...expressed their opinions - that so-called modern or contemporary art cannot be Communist because art in Russia today is realistic and objective...

This glib disavowal of any relationship between communism and...modern art is so pat and so spontaneous a reply by advocates of the 'isms' in art, from deep Red Stalinist to pale pink publicist, as to identify it readily to the observant as that same old party-line practice. It is the party line of the left-wingers, who are now in the big money, and who want above all to remain in the big money, voiced to confuse the legitimate artist, to disarm the arousing academician, and to fool the public . . . From 1914 to 1920 art was used as a weapon of the Russian Revolution to destroy the Czarist Government, but when this destruction was accomplished, art ceased to be a weapon and became a medium of propaganda, picturing and extolling the imaginary wonders, benefits, and happiness of existence under the socialized state . . . The evidence of evil design is everywhere... The question is, what have we, the plain American people, done to deserve this sore affliction that has been visited upon us so direly; who has brought down this curse upon us; who has let into our homeland this horde of germ-carrying art vermin?

GEORGE A. DONDERO

US Congressman
Modern Art Shackled to Communism, 1949

*W*e can say without exaggeration that never has civilization been menaced so seriously as today... We are by no means thinking only of the world war that draws near. Even in times of 'peace', the position of art and science has become absolutely intolerable...

The regime of Hitler, now that it has rid Germany of all those artists whose work expressed the slightest sympathy for liberty, however superficial, has reduced those who still consent to take up pen or brush to the status of domestic servants of the regime, whose task it is to glorify it on order, according to the worst possible aesthetic conventions. If reports may be believed, it is the same in the Soviet Union...

True art...is unable *not* to be revolutionary, *not* to aspire to a complete and radical reconstruction of society... We recognize that only the social revolution can sweep clear the path for a new culture. If, however, we reject all solidarity with the bureaucracy now in control of the Soviet Union, it is precisely because, in our eyes, it represents not communism but its most treacherous and dangerous enemy.

The totalitarian regime of the U.S.S.R....has spread over the entire world a deep twilight hostile to every sort of spiritual value. A twilight of filth and blood... The official art of Stalinism mirrors with a blatancy unexampled in history their efforts to put a good face on their mercenary profession... The *opposition* of writers and artists is one of the forces which can usefully contribute to the discrediting and overthrow of regimes which are destroying, along with the right of the proletariat to aspire to a better world, every sentiment of nobility and even of human dignity.

ANDRE BRETON and **LEON TROTSKY**

Manifesto: Towards a Free Revolutionary Art, 1938

*T*here have been periods which we would like to regard as ideal prototypes of society... Society, had a unified structure, whether communal or hierarchic, and the artist was a member of that society with a definite place and definite function. There was universal faith, and an accepted interplay of authority and function which left the artist with a defined task, and secure position. Unfortunately, our problems are not simplified in that way. We have a society which is fragmented, authority which resides in no certain place, and our function as artists is what we make it by our individual efforts. We live in a transitional age, between one economic structure of society which is in dissolution and another economic order of society which has not yet taken definite shape. As artists, we do not know who is our master... we are individuals seeking patronage, sometimes from an organization of individuals - a public corporation, a museum, an educational authority - sometimes from the State itself. This very diversity of patronage requires, on the part of the modern artist, an adaptability or agility that was not required of the artist in a unified society...

Specialization... may conflict with the particular economic structure of society in which the artist finds himself. Painting and sculpture, for example, might be regarded as unnecessary trimmings in a society committed by economic necessity to an extreme utilitarian form of architecture. The artist might then have to divert his energies to other forms of production; to industrial design, for example. No doubt the result would be the spiritual impoverishment of the society reduced to such extremes, but I only mention this possibility to show the dependence of art on social and economic factors. The artist should realize how much he is involved in the changing social structure, and how necessary it is to adapt himself to that changing structure.

HENRY MOORE

'The Sculptor in Modern Society' read
at a UNESCO meeting, 1952

In all the points so far made about the propaganda value of art there has been a marked emphasis on art in its original sense - meaning visual art, principally painting - as opposed to what Hauser describes as 'other cultural creations'. But the question now to be asked is why. What is so special about paintings that they should have a greater propaganda value for their patrons than plays, music, films, poetry and other creative writing? This is a significant question because it points to the conclusion that art is more political than other cultural creations, and if this is really the case, we need to understand how and why.

Part of the answer lies in the nature of the medium. As John Berger puts it in *Ways of Seeing*:

> What are paintings? Before they are anything else, they are themselves objects which can be bought and owned. Unique objects. A patron cannot be surrounded by music or poems in the same way as he is surrounded by his pictures.

In other words, the objective existence of paintings - their sheer materiality - invests them with a special value for patrons, that of ever-present, permanent prestige. Of course, the same logic holds for the art of the temples and churches or other public monuments, including those created under the patronage of the State. But Berger also points to the value of paintings as commodities, commodities more luxurious than gold on account of their uniqueness and superior to gold because of the cultural and moral authority they extend to their possessors. In this way their propaganda value is twofold. No other form of cultural expression empowers the patron similarly.

One may conclude that, in matters of patronage, paintings are more political than other cultural creations for a further reason, again contingent on their uniqueness. To understand this one must bear in mind that, since the mid-19th century, the intensifying commodification of art and the growth of the international art market have run parallel with another development: the increasing capacity of the general public to support the other arts.

This is not to suggest that public patronage of the other arts has eliminated the need for the bourgeoisie or moneyed elite in their promotion. On the contrary, with the inflation and spiralling costs that are the hallmark of modern capitalism, the publication of books, the production of plays, operas, ballets, music concerts, films, records and so forth have more than ever needed the financial support of the private and corporate sector or of the State. But what is equally obvious is that the people who buy books, tickets, etc. have become of greater and greater importance to the moneyed elite and to those who create 'the goods'. This means it is the public that has the final say when it comes to most forms of cultural expression.

Yet, when it comes to paintings which sell and make the artist a name, the public has no say at all. Their uniqueness has priced them beyond the reach of all but the moneyed elite. It is this more than anything else that gives art its special political significance today. Because successful artists depend on the patronage of the ruling economic elite, their work reflects the mind and tastes of this elite as nothing else can. Even the work of unsuccessful artists - the good ones among them - acknowledges by default the elite's moral and aesthetic standards. In other words, art not only reveals what its patrons are, but also what they are not.

In order to look into the minds of art patrons in contemporary India, a brief word is due on the background and nature of 'the Indian art market'. And the first thing to be said is that, despite the media hype, contemporary Indian art is not an investment in the proper sense of the term. The reason is simple: this country has no organised, regulated market such as exists in the developed world.

The rules governing the international art market have not only evolved over more than a century, they also include fiscal laws designed to encourage the collection and conservation of works of art. Two of the most important of these laws were passed in the early 1950's. Under the first, income-tax relief was extended to any American citizen giving a work of art to an American museum; as an added incentive, the relief was immediate, but the work would go to the museum after the owner's death. The second law was enacted in England: it now became possible to pay death duties with works of art, an incentive that would discourage the export of art. Both pieces of legislation sent art prices rocketing throughout the western world.

The main reason why India has no such laws is that these can only work in a developed, largely white economy. The Indian art market operates within an economy which, despite the changes being wrought by globalisation, is still as much black as white.

A great deal of the art that has been acquired over the post-Independence years by Indian patrons has involved, in part, the exchange of black money. But around the mid-1980's, which marked the beginning of the so-called 'art boom', existing collectors and would-be patrons were handed an opportunity to whiten their money substantially and legally while gaining huge prestige into the bargain. This opportunity came via a clever strategy: the charitable art auction. Auctions of paintings in the name of charity had been held earlier in India but these were relatively low profile and the prices so obtained were modest, even for the big names.

It was the entry into the picture of the auction houses, Christie's and Sotheby's that made the proposition so attractive. It also fooled many into believing that Indian contemporary art had 'arrived on the international scene' a phrase since trotted out with monotonous regularity by the media. However, behind this move lurked shrewd conspirators or power lobbies.

Among the lobbyists were key figures from the art establishment and on its fringes. These included not only artists but also dealers and influential media persons. It was they who would decide which artists would be allowed to benefit from this new opportunity to increase their prices to levels never before dreamed of.

This was a strategy that worked to near perfection. The prices attained at such auctions were higher than anticipated for many artists, and this would enable them henceforward to command much more for their work at exhibitions and through galleries. It would also enable the same artists to continue their domination of the art world to this day.

What it did not, however, achieve was to regularise the art market, even to a minor degree. Indeed, if anything at all, it has further de-regularised it by encouraging behind-the-scenes manipulations and skulduggery. It is beyond the scope of the present argument to give a detailed account of the way the Indian art market works. One only has to remember that there is much more than meets the eye when one reads in the newspapers about the whopping prices occasionally attained for Indian art.

The recent sale of a triptych by Tyeb Mehta for 1.5 crores of rupees was a record for a contemporary artist. But the fact that it was sold abroad is no indication of Indian art's having found acceptance as an investment internationally. Rather, it confirms what has been known for long: that Non-Resident Indians (NRI's) have become important collectors of Indian contemporary art.

21

However, the main reason for which NRI's have sustained interest in this field is the exchange rate between the rupee, the dollar and other major foreign currencies. Since they began collecting around fifteen years ago, they have seen substantial increases in the value of their money in relation to the rupee. Effectively this has meant that they have been able to acquire artworks at the same or lower rates than in the late 1980's, even if the prices in India have increased substantially. This is hardly a manifestation of a flourishing art market.

Broadly speaking, there are two kinds of art that find a market in India. The first is the low-priced commercial art which appeals largely to that section of the moneyed middle-class with little exposure to western culture beyond satellite television. Many of this class do travel abroad but this usually entails little more than shopping expeditions, staying with members of their extended families and conducting conversations in their own language. The pictures or images collected by this class include kitschy reproductions of deities, like those found in the majority of Indian homes, and paintings varying in subject from village scenes and rustic belles, to somewhat modernistic renderings of Lord Ganesha and horses painted in the style of M. F. Husain. It should be noted that many galleries in India survive by selling such paintings. These galleries may at the same time sell what is categorised as 'fine art', which by definition means art primarily concerned with aesthetics.

Talk of 'fine art' brings us to the second category of marketable art in India - the art produced by established names and those who emulate them. And it is here we may encounter the super-moneyed class, the class that can make or break governments. Some call them the de facto rulers of the country. But whatever one may call them, the list of art-collecting tycoons within the country adds up to no more than a few hundred, if one includes their wives and offspring. NRI collectors, who also fit this category, are again relatively few in number.

So what kind of art do these patrons go for? Before answering this, it is essential to note that when it comes to religious imagery, their tastes are generally at one with the middle-class just discussed. Despite or perhaps because of their studies and sojourns abroad, super-rich Indians have remained highly traditional and conservative. Their homes, like those of all orthodox Hindus, have *puja* rooms or family temples and, like them, contain icons of the kitschy variety. These icons may have cost a fortune, made from gold, silver or ivory; but kitsch is kitsch, no matter what it is made of: it is garish and sentimental, a far cry from the great Hindu imagery such as one sees in the ancient monuments.

The art they collect, on the other hand, is of an entirely different order, for it is intended to reflect their liberal, modern, westernised manner and appearance. This has very little to do with subject matter. The paintings that adorn their walls, both at home and at work, can represent almost anything under the sun, including images of gods and goddesses - think again of Husain, or the man who would be Husain, Manjit Bawa. They can also be non-representational or abstract. What fits the modern, westernised image is, therefore, a formal or stylistic question.

In other words, Indian contemporary art must *appear* to be modern irrespective of whether its content is modern or not. And the modern idiom as patrons understand it invariably derives from the language of European modern art. To be noted is the use of the term 'derives from' as opposed to 'being influenced by', an inevitable and desirable development in art resulting from cross-cultural encounters.

What this means in visual terms is not so easy to describe. If one regularly visits exhibitions or galleries dealing in contemporary art, one may discern a great variety of styles or forms of expression. For the layperson, such variety not only causes confusion but also creates the illusion of widespread originality among Indian artists. Moreover, the 'Indian-ness' of so many of the subjects may fool the spectator into believing that the artists responsible are the true sons and daughters of the soil.

We need to ask ourselves how it is apparent that the art acquired by the Indian elite articulates a foreign language a language with a western syntax and grammar and merely an Indian vocabulary. Well, for one thing, at least for the initiate, a lot of Indian contemporary art produces an overwhelming sense of *déjà vu*, the feeling that one has seen it all before. Of course, this by itself does not betray its derivation from western art which, in any case, also often produces the same feeling of *déjà vu*.

What really gives it away is that 'certain modern look', to reduce it to terms normally reserved for fashion. This is, however, quite appropriate since art trends are very much a question of fashion. Like fashion designers, artists often try to make virtue out of the outlandish or gimmicky; this is not the same thing as originality, which is one of the main requirements of art. As Voltaire said:

We must be original without being bizarre.

As to the specifics of 'the look', the art buyer must be able to label images with styles and names like fashion designers' lines or brands in exotic shops. Moreover, in the buyer's eyes, the modern look must not conform to anything vaguely classical. It must appear to break all the rules followed in the past, rules that are still supposed to be imparted to and mastered by students in art college.

This is not to imply for a single moment that the breaking of rules has negative connotations per force. There have been times in history when iconoclasm has been more than necessary. The late 19th century, when modern art was born, marks one of those times. The modern movements across the world, including India, not only contributed hugely to overall intellectual and cultural advances, they also contributed indirectly to political developments like the defeat of fascism and colonialism.

Moreover, while the early modern masters broke classical and academic rules, they remained logical, erecting their new vision on sound theory. And, with the exception of the Dadaists, whose avowed ideology was 'anti-art', they did not turn their backs on the fundamentals of good art by neglecting technique. In other words, they did not throw out the baby with the bath water.

When it comes to mainstream Indian contemporary art, the breaking of rules often follows no other logic than that of disguising technical weaknesses or even crass incompetence. Needless to say, this is of no consequence to patrons. Incapable of discerning quality, all that matters to them is recognisable names. In order for them to collect an artist, they must have heard of her or him, and the more they have heard the name the more compelling it is to acquire her or his work.

As must be obvious, the propagation of an artist's name is largely achieved through the media. There is also a circle of promoters and dealers to support the cause of particular artists. But since there are far more artists than patrons in India, the establishment has space for only a small percentage. So how does an artist join the establishment in order to be publicised and promoted?

The easiest way to become a celebrity artist is to belong to a family that is highly placed either by birth or by dint of power brokering. In a country like India, which is still largely feudal in its politico-social relationships, it is axiomatic that a well-connected family opens doors

25

automatically. It is no less self-evident that those who pay court to the powerful may also enter those doors. In the art world this means that well cultivated friendships and sycophancy can propel an artist onto the rostrum of success.

Another way for an artist to become a big name involves considerable expenditure, compelling him or her to have income from other sources. There was a time when throwing smart parties and wining and dining members of the media was a sufficient formula. But over the last few years, things have come to such a pass that money or expensive gifts are crudely exchanged against coverage, often via an agent, the ubiquitous public relations person.

Once in a blue moon, thanks to an extraordinary stroke of luck, a genuine talent may enter the art establishment with neither the means nor the inclination to pull strings. But once inside, the chances of survival are slim. The sham of the environment and insensitivity of patrons will soon drive the artist away or spell death to his values and talent.

But for those capable of chicanery the rewards are rich. This is not only in terms of selling works, which is far less dependable than the established artists would have us believe. There is also much to be gained from just being a big name, for this means being becoming part of the social set that is written about in the gossip columns of leading dailies. In this way, the artist may rub shoulders with power brokers of all kinds. Of course, the art world itself attracts many power brokers, making it an ideal stamping ground for fixers and climbers. In New Delhi, which tops the list in India as a city of fixers, art is second only to politics for those who aspire for success without cultivating talent.

On a much smaller scale, another kind of art market exists in India. The collectors in this case are mainly drawn from the professional and salaried classes. And among this group are people of genuine cultivation and intellectual curiosity. One can call this the class that constitutes India's real cultural elite.

Of course, most of this elite have limited means and can only afford to buy art on an occasional basis. The work they collect is generally modest in scale and price and is often created by serious artists with no time to waste on the chicanery of the established art world, the world that grabs the attention of the media. The truly discerning collector is equally serious and is least concerned about names and fashion.

Genius, like love, is a word so widely misused in our age of darkness that it has almost ceased to have meaning. This is specially true when people talk of the arts. Scientists are less easily hailed as geniuses than artists and writers because they are first expected to make their mark on the world by creating either something practical or an idea or theory for practical application. Also, their achievements are measured against clearly defined standards. So if someone says that the physicists, Stephen Hawking and S. Chandrashekhar are geniuses, the claim is probably justified because both of them are making revolutionary contributions to our knowledge of the universe, a fact recognised by other scientists.

The identification of genius is far more elusive when it comes to living artists and writers. There can be no dispute if we hail Kalidas, Kabir, Leo Tolstoy, Vincent Van Gogh or Charlie Chaplin as geniuses because, with their own unique vision, they have helped change and enrich people's perceptions of the world. But how can we say the same of the living? Surely, the whole point about names like the above is that they have survived the test of time. In art, what singles out a work of genius from the rest is the capacity to endure.

This means that in order to identify a living genius, a person must have so high a degree of knowledge, sensitivity and perception as to be possessed of prophetic vision. This is an almost impossible virtue to cultivate in an age like ours when we are ceaselessly bombarded with images, information and entertainment, and when success depends on media hype, which means that most of the time we only see, hear or read about the mediocre. How, under such circumstances, can one pinpoint works of genius that will live on?

A more appropriate question to ask is how genius can be cultivated in such an environment. In particular, how can it be cultivated in India where the most degenerate moral and aesthetic values have come to predominate? To answer this, let us turn to an essay, *Waiting for a Genius* by the Chinese writer, Lu Xun. Written in 1924, this was one of his many lucid essays on the cultural crisis engulfing his country, and in it he challenges the widely held notion that a genius appears on earth as though by accident or miracle. This is how he begins:

> Among the many requests shouted at writers and artists today, one of the loudest is the demand for a genius. And this clearly proves two things. First, that there is no genius just now in China; secondly, that everybody is sick and tired of our modern art...

The first thing to strike one about this statement is that it could have been made by a contemporary writer almost anywhere in the world, including India. It is of course true that in India a tiny dilettante elite is convinced it has encountered genius in figures like Arundhati Roy and M.F. Husain. But in the main, the educated in India appear to be sitting back, awaiting the arrival of greatness; either that or they bemoan the fact that the country's greatness lies in the past or that genius is only recognised abroad.

It cannot be denied that there are no figures today comparable to Kalidas and that there is no sign of the artistic genius that contributed to the creation of the great ancient monuments. But what needs to be acknowledged is that a Kalidas or an Ajanta can only come about when society demands them. This is the thrust of Lu Xun's argument. He continues

29

Genius is not some freak of nature which grows of itself in deep forests or wildernesses, but something brought forth and nurtured by a certain type of public... Napoleon once declared, "I am higher than the Alps!" But we must not forget how many troops he had at his back while making this grandiose statement... Before we expect a genius to appear, we should first call for a public capable of producing a genius. In the same way, if we want fine trees and lovely flowers we must have good soil... for without it nothing can grow.

That genius is not heaven-sent but earth-grown is an observation supported by the examples of history. Let us take the case of William Shakespeare or Leonardo da Vinci, considered among the greatest of great minds to have walked the world stage. But how many people have stopped to think how their greatness was achieved?

Even if we assume that they were born prodigies, must we not also acknowledge that their talents would have withered and died had they had no powerful patrons to commission them, no fellow poets or painters to recognise their potentials, no public to which to hold up their achievements to scrutiny and acclaim? As Lu Xun adds towards the end of his essay:

> The first cry of even a genius at birth is the same as that of an ordinary child, it cannot possibly be a beautiful poem.

Let us now look at little closer at the components of the fertile soil from which genius may grow and flourish. Clearly, the richest of these components is the substance known as patronage, which lies on the uppermost layer. One could say this constitutes the topsoil. For Shakespeare this topsoil went by the name of Queen Elizabeth or the Earl of Southampton; for Leonardo it was the Duke of Milan or the King of France. But whatever name they went by, they had one thing in common: they were capable of appreciating excellence. This means they constituted what is known as 'enlightened patronage'.

We should not romanticise the issue. History tells us that patrons of this kind were often far from enlightened when it came to affairs other than art. Elizabeth Tudor may have been Shakespeare's greatest champion, but this hardly prevented her from cutting off the heads of her courtiers or anyone else who crossed her path. And Cesare Borgia, briefly Leonardo's patron, was one of the most monstrous rulers in a very violent age. Moreover, these enlightened patrons nurtured the most talented not merely for pleasure but because they understood that this would enhance their power and prestige and their influence over their subjects, the bottom but most substantial layer of the soil.

The role of the greater public, no matter how uneducated, must never be underestimated in the cultivation of genius. It is after all into this layer of the soil that a plant thrusts its roots to grow tall, strong and enduring. Though both Shakespeare and Leonardo placed the highest value on aristocratic ideals, they asked for and received the recognition of the common populace. They needed their cheers and rotten eggs for the understanding of their strengths and weaknesses and they could always expect great honesty from the crowd. Popular opinion can have been no less important for the creators of the great Indian sacred monuments. Probably for many this constituted the *raison d'être* of their strivings, for they belonged to the people and must have regarded popular appreciation as akin to recognition by their peers.

This brings us to another essential component of the soil. One can hardly find an example in history when a genius has emerged without interacting with his peers and without being recognised by at least a handful of them. Let us not forget that the first person to acknowledge the prodigious talents of Leonardo was his teacher, Andrea del Verrocchio, a versatile master of the highest order and, like his pupil, an artist-scientist. And while Leonardo and Michelangelo hated the sight of one another, they understood and respected each other's powers. The 'half-educated, common player', Will Shakespeare was sometimes plagued by the jealousy of his contemporaries but his talents were also well recognised by them. Besides, he must have enjoyed the esteem of his fellow actors.

Even a genius like Van Gogh, who was cruelly permitted to die for lack of patronage, could achieve what he did thanks in large part to peer recognition. For many of his contemporaries Van Gogh was a god. From recent Indian history we can cite the example of a spoilt genius like Ritwik Ghatak. In worldly terms he was a miserable failure, but he was at least encouraged by fellow artists and intellectuals to complete a small body of outstanding work.

However, we now live in the arid deserts of the present in which no genius can possibly take root. The topsoil is eroded. There is no patronage worth speaking of. Whatever of it there is may be likened to a chemical fertiliser; it is only accessible to already rich farmers; it robs the soil of its natural nutrients; it leads to greater dependency on other imported inputs; it makes the crop vulnerable to pests.

As to peer recognition, this too has eroded. Who among artists is generous and unselfish enough to encourage a superior talent? Most prefer to encourage inferior talents so that their own mediocrity can stand tall. Worse still, most go out of their way to disparage real ability or mastery so that the chances of a genius's flowering are destroyed. In the words of the great 18th century satirist, Jonathan Swift:

> When a true genius appears in the world, you may know him by this sign, that the dunces are all in confederacy against him.

In this situation, the nurturing of genius by the greater public is an impossible option.

If asked to sum up the nature of enlightened art patronage, one could do no better than recall Goethe's rhetorical question:

> What else is barbarism but an incapacity for distinguishing excellence?

But if enlightened patronage means the ability to distinguish excellence, the question to be asked is how excellence works as propaganda. We have already seen that the enhancement of authority and acquisition of prestige have been the motivating force of ruling class art patrons throughout history. And we have further seen that the commodification of art under bourgeois patronage has had undesirable consequences, including the social alienation of the artist and a decline in the moral and aesthetic standards of patrons. The peak of decadence that has been reached in contemporary India has also been discussed.

However, the point we are now looking at is enlightened patronage, as opposed to the barbarism that prevails today. And to understand this better a historic overview of patronage in India prior to colonial rule would be useful.

The logical starting point for such an overview is the age of the Maurya dynasty because it is this dynasty which leaves us with the first concrete records of patronage. At the same time, one must not forget that evidence exists of a strong tradition of patronage in the pre-Mauryan age. There is no guessing the degree of excellence then attained, but we can be certain that the imagery was rooted in folk traditions, meaning that it was highly figurative, sensuous and earthy, giving it enormous popular appeal.

The term 'popular appeal' is of great consequence to our argument. One could sum it up by saying that just as art thrives on enlightened patronage, so the patron derives authority from the uniting power of art. Probably the first Indian ruler to understand this to the full was Ashoka. The monuments and art works attributed to his reign have little to do with the sensuous and celebratory aspects of life. The task before him was an urgent one, and more directly political: to peacefully unite his subjects, over vast and varied territories, through application of the Buddha's special code for kings. His famous rock edicts and columns were not a new form of propagating an ideology; they were clearly inspired by the Iranians, who had once ruled Ashoka's north-west provinces. But in terms of content they were unique. While the edicts represent the world's first bill of human rights, the animal sculptures crowning the columns reflect a softness, affection and respect for all forms of life uncharacteristic of the monumental art of other ancient cultures.

This raises a second point about enlightened patronage. We have already talked about popular appeal, and now we begin to see that the unifying capacity of art is most potent when it upholds humanistic and progressive values. This is not at all to say that popular tastes are a measure of good art, for if this were the case then we would be obliged to admit that today's kitsch is on a par with the great art of the past.

Standards of excellence are set by the real elite, including artists. Enlightened patrons are merely those who recognise and exploit such standards. Moreover, we have already noted that the most degenerate form of 'art' the popular film exerts a unifying power over contemporary Indian society that is unsurpassed by any other force, including religion. The political leadership understands this well and exploits it to the hilt. But this makes leaders shrewd, not enlightened.

If their life depended on it, none of today's leadership - from Messrs. Vajpayee, Advani, Thakeray and Modi to the ideologues of the Vishwa Hindu Parishad (VHP) and the Rashtriya Swayam Sevak Sangh (RSS) - could recognise or define excellence in art. If one placed before them two sacred images from the Golden Age - one a run of the mill work, the other a masterpiece - they would be incapable of making a distinction. And why only the Hindu right? Who among the opposition forces, including members of the so-called 'Left', is anything but a boor? One may cite a possible exception in Sonia Gandhi who has studied art. But it is difficult to imagine that her sensibilities have remained unblunted since she entered politics.

It is important to remember that, from Ashoka's reign on, all the monuments which were constructed and adorned with works of art were strategically placed on or near trade routes. The mercantile classes, together with tribals and cultivators, constituted the majority of the Buddhist faithful, and the reasons were economic as much as social. This may sound obvious, but we need to understand it if we are to reach the heart of enlightened patronage.

After the Buddha's lifetime, trade routes had spread out in every direction, and the early merchant caravans were under constant threat of attack by hostile local tribes. What they needed were protectors who had won the locals' confidence, and they found them in Buddhist monks. This is because trade routes had been developed from the prehistoric tracks trodden for millennia by tribespeople. And in accordance with the rules laid down by the Buddha, members of the monastic order had followed these tracks carrying his message of peace and equality, halting at cult spots frequented by the locals.

It was in these places that monasteries were established and it was here that merchants found shelter and protection. In return, they donated generously to the monasteries, providing the means to build permanent structures and to enlarge and beautify them with sculpture and painting. These are the origins of all the archaeological monuments connected with Buddhism and they span a period of almost a millennium. Among these sites were the *stupas* at Barhut, Sanchi, Bodh Gaya, Sarnath, Mathura and Amaravati, and the excavated cave sanctuaries at Karle, Kondane, Aurangabad and Ajanta.

Merchants were not, of course, the only patrons of Buddhist art. Most if not all of these sacred monuments enjoyed royal patronage, some of it coming from tribal or *Naga* kings and queens. And by no means all royal patrons were Buddhist.

Patrons also emanated from many other social classes, as D.D. Kosambi makes clear. In *The Culture and Civilisation of Ancient India*, he records that among those to contribute to the creation of Karle (circa 1st century) were: bankers, high officials, a merchants' union, guilds of bamboo workers, braziers, potters, a Greek physician, a blacksmith, a scribe, a carpenter, a head fisherman, the wife of a ploughman and the mother of a household farmer.

Inscriptions at Barhut (circa 2nd century BC) also prove that within only a few centuries of the Buddha's death, monks and nuns had accumulated sufficient individual wealth to finance works of art. Needless to say, this was in flagrant violation of monastic rules.

Enlightened patronage? Of this there can be no doubt, despite or because of the breaking of the Buddha's law. Importantly, it was not only with respect to individual property that monastics turned away from their founder. As Madanjeet Singh notes in his book, *Ajanta*, the Buddha had also ordained that representational art was unsuitable for the eyes of those who had joined the order. With clear reference to the images then painted on the chamber walls of the ruling elite, the Buddha decreed:

> Monks, you should not have a bold design made with the figures of women, figures of men...

Yet it was precisely such images that were sculpted and painted in profusion at *stupas* and cave sanctuaries across the land from around the 2nd century BC.

Why had this come about? Clearly these art works were not the ancient Indian equivalent of naughty peep shows created as a diversion from the austere life of monks. No, the answer is obvious when we recall the lists of donors and when we remember that these sacred sites were places of pilgrimage, places where people not necessarily of the faith would learn about the Buddha's life and ideals.

So we now return full circle to the question of popular appeal. Religious leaders, when they are successful, are always politically astute. And the Buddhist hierarchy of that time was probably more astute than most. Witnessing the phenomenal strength of their founder's message, they soon understood that they could draw and hold large numbers, not by homilies delivered by the elders, but through an attractive language familiar to the people. If this is not a mark of enlightened patronage, then nothing is. And it is something totally lacking in the religious leadership of today, whatever denomination that leadership may represent.

After the disintegration of the Mauryan empire, the first important art patrons were the Satavahana, the dynasty that originated in the Deccan. During their rule, trade in this region expanded hugely, not only with the rest of India but also with Rome. The Romans had established settlements on both the peninsular coasts, and Indian luxury goods like textiles, precious stones and spices were exchanged for gold. The fabulous wealth so accumulated paved the way for the flowering of a sophisticated urban culture. The court languages were Sanskrit and its simpler cousin, Prakrit; the earliest Prakrit literature developed under their patronage and, as Kosambi further notes, at least one of this dynasty, King Hala, was a poet of accomplishment. Though the Satavahana were devotees of Krishna, it was to the Buddhist monasteries that they extended patronage. Among the marvels created under their rule (circa 50 BC-250 AD) are some of the early Ajanta caves, the gateways of the Sanchi *stupa* and the *stupas* at Amaravati and Nagarjunkonda in Andhra Pradesh.

In approximately the same era, the northern subcontinent was ruled by the Central Asian Kushana dynasty. Like most of the rulers who settled here before the British, the Kushana integrated quickly with Indian society through marriage alliances and the adoption of local deities and customs, at the same time invigorating the local culture with new ideas and practices. With political and trade links extending from China to Rome, the Kushana empire became a dynamic cultural confluence, a meeting point of Indian, Chinese, Greco-Roman and Zoroastrian thought. The first Sanskrit drama developed under them, some of it incorporating Greek stories into the plot.

The most eminent of this dynasty was Kanishka I, a devout Buddhist, and the spread of Buddhism to China via missionaries and trade links is largely attributed to his reign. Evidently inspired by the example of Ashoka, Kanishka commissioned the construction and embellishment of *stupas* and monasteries across his territories. He was also instrumental to the blossoming of two great centres of art - Mathura and Gandhara - and these continued to receive support under his successors. So great was the impact of Kushana patronage at Mathura that the style developed here in this era bears the name of this dynasty.

Kanishka was also the first recorded Indian ruler to assemble scholars of diverse disciplines and his court must have shone with intellectual brilliance. Among the minds associated with his reign were: the poet-dramatist, Asvaghosha; the philosopher Nagarjuna, one of the chief exponents of Mahayana Buddhism; and the physician, Charaka, author of the first compendium of Indian medical science.

The example of Kanishka highlights another dimension of enlightened patronage: support to cultural and intellectual endeavour of all kinds, above all the scientific. For rarely in world history has there been a time when the arts flourished and science was in the wilderness, and vice versa. The two have always needed each other, and the ruling elite to realise this has been all the wiser.

The Gupta emperors and aristocracy, the most illustrious of Indian art patrons, were clearly not wanting in this regard. While living in the utmost luxury, they financed free hospitals for the general public and extended support to the advancement of medical science. This was also an age of advancement in mathematics. The chief exponent of 'the Indian art', as the Arabs would later call it, was Aryabhat, also an astronomer. In addition to compiling the first treatise on decimal notation, Aryabhat postulated the theory that the earth revolves around the sun.

To some it seems strange that these achievements coincided with the age of the *Kama Sutra*. But those familiar with this treatise on the art of love will be well aware that it is much more than a sex manual. Written for the sophisticated urban male, a lot of it is devoted to the refinements he should cultivate in his quest not only for pleasure but also to be a pleasing lover. The practice of painting is one of these refinements. With a ruling elite of this kind, can we wonder that this was an age of enlightenment.

Chandragupta II (circa 375-415 AD) is of course remembered as the most cultivated of the Gupta monarchs. Like Kanishka, he gathered at his court the finest artists and men of letters, almost certainly including Kalidas. And like Kanishka, he ensured that his dynastic name would be immortalised by a style of art. It is well known that the Gupta emperors supported places of worship of every sect, while they themselves were staunch devotees of Vishnu. But it needs to be underlined that the very finest of all sculptures anywhere in the world portraying the Buddha carry their name. These were mainly the product of Sarnath and Mathura. Some of Ajanta's finest murals also have Gupta associations; Chandragupta II's daughter ruled the Deccan after the death of her husband and she was evidently as enlightened a patron as her father.

It would be a useless exercise to dwell at any length on the celebrated patron dynasties that succeeded the above. By now the general points have been made about what constitutes enlightenment in a ruling elite. At the same time, no roll call of this kind can be complete without mentioning the Chalukya and Pallava who dominated South India at varying periods between the 4th and 9th centuries. The cultural developments that occurred under their rule followed a similar pattern: the adoption of Sanskrit as a court language and the evolution of their own language, respectively Kannada and Tamil.

As art patrons the Chalukya name is associated with the twilight years of Ajanta and the first great temples dedicated to Shiva at Elephanta, Ellora, Badami and Aihole. As to the Pallavas, in the whole of Indian ancient art history there is nothing to compare for intimate delight with the rock-cut shore temples at Mahabalipuram. Eclectic in spirit and unfussy in style, they are the gems in the crown of the classical age that began with the Guptas.

Pallava art and culture travelled far and wide, exerting huge influence in today's Kampuchea, Vietnam and Malaysia. Perhaps nothing sums up the spirit of their times than the title of a play attributed to one of their kings, *The Delight of the Drunkards*. Surely this tells us something further about enlightened rulers - that they are neither puritanical nor hypocritical. This is something to think about in today's India.

If one were to undertake a survey abroad among people with a fair level of cultural education, and if one were to ask them to identify India's most illustrious patron dynasty, most of them would come up with the name 'Mughal'.

The great repute of this dynasty is undoubtedly justified although it needs to be put into perspective. Whatever the RSS and VHP may say, Akbar and Jahangir were probably no less enlightened than their Gupta counterparts. But it is also true that the art produced under them had less social significance than Gupta art because it was not intended for the gaze of the public. Only their architecture fulfilled this role.

Does this mean that the best of Mughal miniature paintings and illustrated manuscripts were less great than the finest Ajanta mural paintings or Gupta sculptures? It depends what we mean by greatness. As Germaine Greer points out, greatness in art is often judged by its dimension and ability to overwhelm. In *The Obstacle Race*, a history of women artists, she says:

> *Great* art, for those who insist on this rather philistine concept (as though un-great art were unworthy of even their most casual and ill-informed attention), makes us stand back and admire. It rushes upon us pell-mell...or towers above us.

She goes on to talk about a more intimate kind of art which reinforces human dignity. This can certainly be said about the finest of Mughal art, and in this sense we can probably call it great. What is meant by the finest is another question and a very important one, but it is beyond the scope of the present argument.

One of the most important aspects of Mughal patronage was its secular character. It is not that in earlier epochs all art was sacred. On the contrary, according to evidence elsewhere examined in detail, secular traditions flourished in ancient India, though these are generally ignored by historians. But the point about the Mughals is that we see for the first time the emergence of a full-fledged secular tradition. They did of course commission the illustration of many sacred texts but, for obvious reasons connected to Islam, these were intended for study and pleasurable perusal rather than worship. With his curiosity about other faiths, the illiterate Akbar commissioned many such works.

As noted by S.A.A. Rizvi in *The Wonder That Was India (Volume II)*, during the exile of his father, Humayun in Iran, Akbar had studied art under the respected master, Abudu's-Samad. It is recorded that, although he neglected his formal lessons, the young prince enjoyed painting. Later, this experience must have helped to make him more discerning than the average ruler.

But it was his son Jahangir who was the patron supreme of the Mughal dynasty. So discerning was his eye that he could recognise the brushwork of each of the many masters attached to his court. Under him, secular themes and genres became predominant. Animals, birds and plants were popular subjects and they were depicted with great skill, realism and affection for nature. Portraiture above all was favoured, and this genre became very elaborate. In many portraits the emperor is surrounded by numerous courtiers, finely detailed, each with individual features and demeanour.

Self-glorification no doubt motivated Jahangir and in this he was no different from other powerful rulers whether Indian, Chinese, European or other. But on the other side, there are numerous works created in his reign reflecting the life of ordinary people, including wandering holy men, soldiers, musicians, artisans, villagers and labourers. And all of them are portrayed with the same loving care and eye for detail as the emperor.

Mughal miniature painting initially was a fusion of Persian and indigenous, mainly Rajput, elements. But, by Jahangir's reign, artistic contacts with Europe had made their mark. The modelling of figures to create roundness, lost since the Ajanta period, was reintroduced, and perspective was introduced into compositions for the first time.

Without doubt the finest works of the Mughal school stand up to their European counterparts. And there can be little doubt that had colonialism not dealt a deathblow to indigenous endeavour, India's art tradition would have achieved new heights under patronage other than Mughal. For a considerable time, the Pahari princes filled the void left by the declining Mughals. But Pahari miniatures do not carry the Mughal tradition forward, they simply maintain it. This is not to say that they fail to work their own kind of magic. They are lyrical and sensuous, qualities that fit the narrative they illustrate, often focused on literary themes like the amorous exploits of Krishna. The high point of many Pahari miniatures is landscape; in some of them, the forms and colours of nature are rendered with such intense delight that the themes appear to have been mere pretexts for the artists.

All of this brings us to a very major difference between miniature paintings and the European art of the same age. This has nothing to do with reduced scale and it applies to all schools of miniature painting. This difference lies in the critical element so often discernible in the works of the European masters. Miniature paintings did not always depict happy themes; the dark and grotesque sides of life were not ignored. But this is not the same thing as a critical questioning of accepted beliefs or of life itself, such as we see in the works of, say, Rembrandt.

Why should this be so? Is it because in India there was little to criticise? Common sense and our history books tell us otherwise. No, the real reason is that India at that time was still largely feudal whereas Europe was well on the way to becoming a capitalist society.

It would be wrong to assume that the critical element is absent in Indian miniatures simply because, under feudal rule, nobody dared question the existing order. This is also because artists at the court of the Mughals or hill princes were not thrown to the wolves as happened to Rembrandt. Let it be remembered that this extraordinary artist was declared bankrupt and died in penury; later Wolfgang Amadeus Mozart would meet the same grisly end.

As already implied, art in Europe acquired its fully secular character under capitalism. The transition was more rapid in Germany, England and Holland, where the Protestant movement had forced a separation from the Roman Catholic Church. The term 'secular art' in the age under reference does not at all signify that artists then ceased to depict religious subjects. Rather, it signifies a change in the nature of patronage: this passes from pope and Church hierarchy, to king and aristocracy, to bourgeois industrialist class. Consumption patterns also change: from public or collective to private or individual.

If the secularisation of art in Europe was a capitalist development, is it not possible that the secular art produced under the Mughals heralded a new socio-economic order? Is it in fact true that the Mughal artists worked in an entirely feudal set up? There is evidence to suggest that just prior to colonisation India had undergone upheavals which had laid the ground for an industrial revolution.

According to S.K. Ghosh in *The Indian Big Bourgeoisie*, the changes that had taken place towards this end were: a trend towards private property; monetisation of the urban economy; a marked growth of productive forces; and the expansion of towns and cities. However, he also believes that the social developments which occurred concurrently were more important than the economic. As he underlines:

> The question is not really one of industrial revolution but of the social revolution that smashes the old production relations which

act as a brake on the development of the productive forces that have already emerged within the old society.

In drawing this conclusion, Ghosh cites peasant revolts, a loosening of the caste system and religious reform movements as symptoms of the social revolution that transpired under Mughal rule.

Insofar as art is concerned, there appears to have been a definite trend towards the emergence of the individual during this era. Two things support this observation. Firstly, from Akbar's time, the names of artists began to be recorded systematically, and under Jahangir the list is exhaustive. Secondly, and more importantly, Jahangir's patronage gave rise to the emergence of individual styles and painters working in specialised subjects.

Jahangir's name has cropped up so often and so favourably in the foregoing discussion that one might be tempted to set him on too high a pedestal. But kings, like everyone else, belong to a time and place and some are dealt a very lucky hand. Jahangir had the luck to rule at a time when the empire was consolidated and relatively peaceful, leaving him free to pursue his artistic interests and bring glory to his name. This was often the case with the second or third of a powerful dynastic line.

It is certainly true that, as an art patron, Jahangir was the last and greatest of the so-called 'Great Mughals'. Though most of his artists remained at the court of his son, Shahjahan, his passing marked the beginning of stagnation and decline. It would be almost three hundred years before this trend was reversed. By that time a foreign empire had come and almost gone.

*The artist is the conscience keeper of society,
the visionary sorcerer, whose task it is
to exorcise evil by whatever means . . .*

*Anil Karanjai
Indian artist and intellectual*

Right from the time that people became people, they have always needed art. Science has known for long that one of the principle characteristics or abilities distinguishing our species, *homo sapiens*, from our ancestor, *homo erectus*, was the articulation of language - a language which was visual as much as oral. In more recent times, experts have begun to recognise that communication through images played a much more important role in human evolution than previously believed.

The demand for art by *homo sapiens* has been a much debated issue. Over the years, archaeologists, anthropologists and other experts have propounded several theories on the motivations underlying cave or rock art. These include: magic and shamanism; religion and totemism; sexuality and fertility rites; communication and ceremonial symbolism; calendar devices and secular records; decoration and doodling. But whatever the polemics of the debate, it is now generally agreed that rock art served different purposes at different stages of our species' development and that its purpose also varied according to the kind of images represented.

Many of the early discoveries of rock art were made in the deep, dark interiors of European caves, as opposed to the more open rock shelters of warmer climes like the African and Indian. This and the dominance of the colonising cultures ensured that the study of rock art was initially Eurocentric to say the least. Consider, for example, that the earliest discovery of an Indian Stone Age painting was made prior to the discovery of European cave sites like Altamira in Spain, world renowned for their paintings of bulls and other large animals. The Indian painting was ignored because the colonial administration declined to believe that it was thousands of years old. Since all Indian art and culture was primitive in their eyes, the painting was officially attributed to tribals of no earlier than the 16th century.

Today, such absurd prejudices are no longer countenanced by science but there remain huge grey areas in the corpus of knowledge on the subject of global rock art. India and the rest of South Asia are among the regions where rock art studies are still very young. While this holds out the possibility of exciting discoveries, it implies that caution must be exercised in drawing conclusions about Indian rock art and its functions.

Nobody urged more caution in this matter than Vishnu S. Wakankar, a pioneer of Indian rock art studies. In his book, *Stone Age Painting in India*, when discussing the probable reasons for the existence of rock art, he observes that

> the answers for India are almost certain to be eclectic.

He bases this view on the great number and variety of rock paintings in the region and on the very long time span over which they were created.

An artist as well as an archaeologist, Wakankar believed that from the earliest ages

> the need for creativity, or art for art's sake, has been part of the genetic make-up of some individuals in all cultures…

He also believed it possible that there were people in those times who enjoyed and appreciated works of art. The high artistic quality of many rock art images in different global regions, including India, seems to confirm Wakankar's view that, aside from its other functions, art has always served an aesthetic purpose. However, as we shall see later on, aesthetics is closely linked to utility. This is particularly true of very early cultures in which the beautiful was often defined precisely as the useful.

Experts of the subject generally agree that, of all rock art's functions, the most consequential were those of magic and animistic religion. Most experts further agree that the magical and religious functions of rock art tended to overlap. This means we can talk in terms of the 'magico-religious' or of ritualised magic.

At the same time, there are important distinctions between the magical and religious functions of art. As Wakankar interprets it:

> Magic is the manipulation of objects, images, symbols, and rituals to produce a specific and immediate result. It is less designed to propitiate the object of fear than to command success in overcoming it. It is less concerned with awe, reverence, and worship than with killing an antelope.

In its literal sense, magic as we know it today is the art of illusion, a mere diversion. But for the hunters of the Old Stone Age, called by experts the Upper Palaeolithic Age, magic was essential to survival. This because it provided the means to acquire power over nature. The depiction of an animal before a hunt was designed to ensure the hunt's success. Based on the belief that to portray something is to possess it, this practice was not merely based on primitive superstition. It also evolved from empirical knowledge: here was a formula that worked, and it was effective because it empowered both the individual and the collective. Ernst Fischer explains why:

> The frenzied tribal dances before a hunt really did increase the tribe's sense of power... Cave

48

paintings of animals really helped to build up the hunter's sense of security and superiority over his prey... Man, the weak creature, confronting dangerous, incomprehensible, terrifying Nature, was greatly helped in his development by magic.

Fisher goes on to point out that at later stages in human evolution magic became differentiated into religion, science and art. This is a vastly important observation because it highlights the three broad spheres of the human psyche from which spring action: belief, knowledge and creativity. In this sense we can say that magic lies at the foundation of our civilisation. Equally we can say that it lies at the very core of our individual existence. Another way of putting this is that there is something of the magician in each of us.

With all this in mind, let us consider the remainder of Fischer's argument on art and magic:

> True as it is that the essential function of art for a class destined to change the world is not that of making magic but of enlightening and stimulating action, it is equally true that a magical residue in art cannot be entirely eliminated, for without that minute residue of its original nature, art ceases to be art. In all the forms of its development, in dignity and fun, persuasion and exaggeration, sense and nonsense, fantasy and reality, art always has a little to do with magic. Art is necessary in order that man should be able to recognize and change the world, but art is also necessary by virtue of the magic inherent in it.

One really cannot escape Fischer's conclusion that art is only art when it works magic. No matter what the genre, no matter how humdrum, commonplace or unpleasant the subject, a work of art is comparable to the conjuror's trick say, pulling rabbits from a hat - because it makes us wonder how it was achieved, it gives us cause for surprise, it opens our eyes to something new. A few examples are needed to illustrate this perception. Two or three works by Picasso immediately come to mind.

The first is *Guernica* (Plate 4), unarguably Picasso's most famous painting, created in response to the bombing of the ancient Basque capital in 1937 by the Nazis. Although Picasso always insisted that *Guernica* was symbolic and not political, the work assumed great political significance. One of the reasons for this is that, throughout Generalissimo Francisco Franco's dictatorship (1938-75), many Spaniards hid postcard sized reproductions of it as symbols of hope and freedom. But reproductions, no matter how fine, can never match the impact - the magic - of the original.

Since *Guernica* was commissioned by the Republican Government as a mural, it was executed on a vast scale. This alone does not account for its impact for, as already noted, greatness in art has little to do with size. But in *Guernica* size combines with another factor, colour, or rather the absence of colour; Picasso chose to paint the whole work in monochrome, giving it the effect of a mammoth newspaper cartoon. This serves to heighten its brutal irony. The sheer pain and terror conveyed by the human and animal figures come across with such force as to leave one spellbound. Then the question arises: how did he do it, how does he make us feel the terror and pain? A magical experience is by no means always pleasant.

But in two of Picasso's small bronze sculptures we do experience a delightful kind of magic. The first is a bull's head (Plate 6) and the second a baboon with her baby. What makes these works magical is that they have been transformed from other objects: the horned bull's head is cast from an upturned bicycle saddle and handlebars; the baboon's head is cast from a toy car that belonged to the artist's small son. In front of both these works one experiences child-like wonder.

Magic and art are both concerned with the metamorphosis of matter, the transformation of objects or entities from one medium to another; Picasso understood this better than anyone. Indeed, he thought of himself as a 'primitive' sorcerer, like those who created the bulls at Altamira. The legend of Picasso, the magician, began early in his career. This is why he is so very apt an example when we talk of art and its magical foundations.

In the context of contemporary Indian art there is a further reason for the aptness of Picasso's example. This is the frequency with which his name is taken when the focus of attention is Maqbool Fida Husain. In fact, quite early in his career, Husain acquired a reputation as 'the Indian Picasso'. This is a reputation that needs to be scrutinised if for no other reason than that Husain is now a household name in India and the sole artist-icon India has produced since Amrita Shergil. Of course, he largely owes his iconic status to his relatively recent association with Madhuri Dixit and the world of films. But whatever the reason for it, an icon he has become, and it is precisely on this account that his public persona needs to be examined. In India, icons are worshipped with far greater fervour than in most other cultures, simply because they are icons. No thought is given to the example they set, whether they are worthy of respect and emulation.

If one is to compare Husain to Picasso, the first thing to ask whether or not the former, like the latter, is a magician. This is a very big question because it calls for an overall assessment of his talents and his contribution to Indian art.

Magical experiences in front of works of art are also experiences of feelings or emotions. Moreover, as will become clear later on when looking at the science of aesthetics, an artwork is not art unless it communicates feeling. Exactly the same point has already been made about magic.

In applying this logic to Husain, one must admit that he does possess sleight of hand, a term generally associated with magic. He has never lost the skill he acquired in his early years, when he painted giant billboards advertising films. His bold lines, his keen sense of colour, composition and design, and his ability to work swiftly under the public gaze all developed from this experience. Moreover, he must be credited with being one of the first Indian artists to integrate the language of European modern art with Indian subjects.

But does Husain's sleight of hand make him a magician, an artist capable of expressing and communicating feelings? The answer to this question is affirmative almost entirely in relation to the past. Once, long ago, Husain did have a magical touch, he did possess the means to stimulate emotional responses in his viewers. But for about forty years he has merely repeated himself. His work may have changed from time to time in subject and detail, but in form and content it has remained as it was when he was a young artist, minus the freshness and originality. It is as though he never dared go beyond his original achievements, never dared to be anything but a brand. A Husain has always had to look like a Husain in case somebody fails to recognise it. This is the mark of somebody interested in image, not of a truly creative spirit.

At the same time, as already noted, Husain's sleight of hand or conjuring skill has not been lost. His work is still sometimes very charming. But it charms in the superficial sense of the term. It does not work magic in the way outlined above; it neither makes us wonder how he did it nor surprises us with the power of his imagination. Only those foolish or innocent enough to be beguiled will deem otherwise.

As to 'the Indian Picasso', one can only say that this comparison has been made in ignorance of Picasso's prodigious talents and of his immense contribution to people's ways of seeing across the globe. Of course, Husain's big success story is one of the reasons for the comparison. But to put this in proper perspective, let us consider for a moment the words of John Berger. On the subject of the Spanish master he says:

> Other artists have courted success, adapted themselves to society, betrayed their beginnings. Picasso has done none of these things. He has invited success as little as Van Gogh invited failure.

The same cannot be said of Husain. As a young artist he may have had a few lucky breaks he did not consciously seek, but he can otherwise be firmly grouped with Berger's 'other artists'. Almost without exception, successful Indian artists have played the right game in the right places, have turned their backs on the creative and ideological principles they may once have held. But few have done these things as thoroughly as Husain, particularly in the matter of betraying their beginnings. Unlike Picasso, who was of lower middle-class background, Husain's origins are really humble.

It is of interest to note that the above Berger quotation is drawn from his book, *The Success and Failure of Picasso*. This is a masterpiece of critical writing which, as the title makes clear, deals with the contradictions in the artist's work and life. Let us consider one of Berger's insights into Picasso's failure:

> Art is the nearest to an oracle that our position as modern scientific men can allow us. What happens to an artist's gifts may well reveal...

what is happening to his contemporaries. The fate of Van Gogh was the partial fate of millions.... And so it is with Picasso. The waste of his genius, or the frustration of his gifts, should be a fact of great significance for us. Our debt to him and to his failures, if we understand them properly, should be enormous.

As already underlined, Husain's gifts were never anywhere near as prodigious as Picasso's, but we can apply Berger's logic to the former in every other respect. A case study of Husain should indeed be of great significance for us and we should also be indebted to him if we properly understand his failures - how and why he squandered his talent and compromised his integrity.

For the moment, another question arises: why is it so useful for us to understand Husain if he is not a giant like Picasso? The answer is that the former, like the latter, has been the representative of a society - a society with a particular politico-economic order, at a particular moment in history. So Husain's case, too, is of an oracular nature; he too reflects a great deal about that order and about the failure of his society.

In order to grasp this properly, we need to constantly remind ourselves that the kind of society in which Picasso lived and worked differed considerably from Husain's. Though Picasso was born in a still largely feudal Spain, he spent most of his life as a political exile in a ripened capitalist world. Husain, on the other hand, represents a complex, highly contradictory culture: a former colony yearning to emulate the white man's society, yet unable to rid itself of the rigid feudalism underlying its politico-economic and social structure.

No matter what his talents or character, Husain could never have been a Picasso on account of these differences. To be Picasso one would need to have been born into his society

54

and his time. This may sound like a statement of the obvious, but in fact it needs to be underscored. This is because there are far too many western educated Indians who have fooled themselves into believing that their world differs little from that of the Europeans and that they can, therefore, aspire to the life and rewards offered by that society without compromising their integrity. Artists are among the most fervid adherents of this belief.

Picasso's failure - in fact, a tragedy - was that he became an icon in a grand bourgeois society whereas he was temperamentally built and driven to represent ordinary, simple people. This is why most of the time he did not know what to paint and why, in consequence, he painted a great deal of rubbish. Of this, of course, he was supremely conscious. As he said in an interview:

> The people no longer seek consolation in art.
> But the refined people, the rich, the idlers seek
> the new, the extraordinary, the extravagant,
> the scandalous. I have contented these people
> with all the many bizarre things that come into
> my head. And the less they understand, the
> more they admire it.

When he joined the Communist Party in 1944, this was not merely to cock a snook at the bourgeoisie; there was also a genuine desire in him to work for a cause. For the Communists, catching Picasso was a great propaganda coup. But Stalinist policy dictated that modern art was bourgeois, reactionary and decadent, so the Party was unable to exploit his genius. This 'failure of revolutionary nerve', as Berger describes it, was to intensify Picasso's sense of tragic isolation.

There is nothing tragic about Husain. The betrayal of his background and artistic beginnings does not appear to have remotely bothered him. But among the things we can understand from his example is that in independent India it has been impossible for an artist from an ordinary background to succeed without falling over backwards to please the powers that be. One may cite the odd exception such as Ganesh Pyne, but such exceptions only serve to prove the rule.

Yet pleasing the powers that be is the very antithesis of the role assigned to the artist since the days of the Stone Age. This is the role of the magician, who brings and holds the community together by dint of his creative powers, knowledge and wisdom.

In a modern context, there are two distinct aspects to this role. The first relates to the artist's work - what he or she creates and the degree of commitment brought to it. The second is concerned with the artist's responsibility as a social and political being. Of course, the two areas sometimes overlap but in the main they should not be confused. It has to be stressed time and again that ideology expressed in works of art is neither an excuse for technical incompetence nor a substitute for commitment in life.

When one talks of celebrities, clear distinctions must be made between the public persona and private individual. What somebody is or does in private should be nobody's business unless the individual concerned makes his or her private life a public spectacle or if the public is affected by the individual's conduct.

A further point to be clarified is that, like it or not, everyone on this planet is a political being. And because artists occupy a privileged position in society, they have a greater responsibility than others. The assertion that an artist has the right to be apolitical simply does not hold weight because to profess this is to acquiesce in the established order, which is imperfect at best and at worst severely repressive. At the same time, the artist's responsibility as a political and social being does not compel him to be a revolutionary or even an activist. What it does demand is exemplary behaviour in the professional arena.

With regard to Picasso it should be noted that in the strict sense of the term he was not what is called 'a political animal'. His joining the Communist Party was a search for a cause and a channel for his talents. It was also in part an emotional response to the war years and the Nazi occupation of France. At the time of his joining, he described his feelings as follows:

> Have not the Communists been the bravest in France... and in my own Spain? How could I have hesitated? The fear to commit myself? But on the contrary I have never felt freer, never felt more complete. And then I have been so impatient to find a country again: I have always been an exile, now I am no longer one...

Husain by comparison has been a lucky man for he has never had to live in exile. True, he was born into a land under foreign occupation but repressive as the British were, they did not go around making lists of degenerate artists and threatening their lives. However, had they done so, it is hardly possible to believe that Husain would have acted with the kind of steadfastness demonstrated by Picasso during the German occupation of France.

Despite being considered by Hitler the most degenerate of artists, Picasso stayed in Paris throughout the war, having turned down offers of asylum in the United States and Mexico. Moreover, he remained unfazed by the Gestapo raids on his apartment. During one such raid, an official espied a photograph of *Guernica* and asked the artist if he had done it. Picasso shot back with his famous terse reply in which he placed the responsibility for *Guernica* on the officer and his fellow Nazis. But one should not overestimate Picasso's courage. He must have been well aware that his status as an international celebrity afforded him protection, even from the likes of Hitler and the Gestapo.

However, in much less threatening circumstances - Indira Gandhi's Emergency - Husain not only remained silent, like most liberal intellectuals, he also played the courtier. He had for long been a protégé of the Nehru family so his passive acquiescence was not unexpected. But what did surprise many was his act of sycophancy when he painted Mrs. Gandhi as the Goddess Durga.

The communal riots ensuing from the destruction of the Babri Masjid presented an opportunity for Husain to take a stand on the side of the people. This might have been expected because the fiercest riots took place in the city that had nurtured him, the erstwhile Bombay. The fact that he professes to be a practising Muslim and that the majority of the victims were from this community may possibly have raised expectations further. These were, however, to be dashed. Apart from a few vague statements in the media about the culpability of politicians in general, Husain's sole public response to these monstrous events was to exhibit an installation called *Violence* in the National Gallery of Modern Art.

Violence consisted of a hurriedly assembled black tent, in the centre of which hung white panels, each adorned with childish scribbles and splashes of blood-red paint. This was hardly for the first or last time that an Indian artist has alluded to politics in art in order to avoid taking a political stand that might anger the powers that be. But Husain is a

58

leader, and cultural leaders are expected to behave with greater responsibility and sensitivity. It would have been better had he done nothing than to create something as shoddy as *Violence.*

In *Art and Revolution*, John Berger makes a pertinent point about the role of today's artist:

> When the social position of the artist was that of an artisan or a super-craftsman, the spirit of competition acted as a stimulus. Today the position of the artist has changed. He is no longer valued as the producer of his work, but for the quality of his vision and imagination as expressed in his work. He is no longer primarily a maker of art: he is an example of a man, and it is his art which exemplifies him.

Art and Revolution is about the Russian sculptor, Ernst Neizvestny who became an example of a man by confronting Khrushchev with such audacity that he risked being killed or sentenced to hard labour in Siberia. This was at a time when artists in the Soviet Union were still firmly in the grip of Stalinist policy. Not long after the confrontation this policy was considerably relaxed, an illustration of what may be achieved by a fearless cultural leader.

Probably aware of how history would judge him, Picasso said in an interview about a decade before his death:

> Today, as you know, I am famous and very rich. But when I am alone with myself, I

haven't the courage to consider myself an artist, in the great and ancient sense of that word.... I am only a public entertainer, who understands his age.

Husain has been known to refer to himself as an entertainer but he has never come out with so unpretentious a statement. Like Picasso he has often averred that his patrons understand nothing of art. But unlike him he has never been a candid self-critic, admitting to have become famous by contenting them with the outlandish, gimmicky and nonsensical.

A large part of the responsibility for Husain's conceit must be borne by the media. We hardly need reminding that the media everywhere is celebrity obsessed and that cultural icons are a special draw. But while the media elsewhere allows for dissent, giving coverage to worthwhile anti-establishment figures, the Indian media protects the interests of the established, in most cases because they have their own interests to protect. One may cite for instance the *India Today* and *The Times of India* groups, both of which are involved in marketing art. Editors in general toe the line either because they are too busy carving a political career or because they rub shoulders with celebrity artists at the top events on the politico-social calendar.

In 1870, the French Realist painter, Gustave Courbet, a close associate of Baudelaire, declined the Cross of the Legion of Honour awarded by his government. In a letter to the Minister of Fine Arts he wrote:

At no time, in no case should I have accepted it. Still less should I accept it today, when treason multiplies itself on all sides and human conscience cannot but be troubled at so much self-seeking and disloyalty.... My conscience as an artist is no less repelled by accepting a reward which the hand of the Government is pressing upon me. The State is not competent in artistic matters.

Courbet's words ring so freshly that they could have been written almost anywhere in today's world but many will feel that they have a special resonance in India. In fact the parallels are so obvious that they barely need elaboration. The only point that needs to be made is that in refusing state honours Courbet was acting as the conscience-keeper of society, one of the main roles of the artist. Moreover, his words imply that to fulfil this role, the artist must be anti-establishment, even if he is a well established name.

It would be ridiculous to suggest that this is an easy role to take on. It requires the artist to be made of steel, to be ready to sacrifice awards, commissions and sales, to risk angering and being cold-shouldered by the powers that be. In Courbet's case, his sacrifice did not end with refusing state honours; he participated in the revolutionary Paris Commune and after its fall he was forced into exile, never to return to France. Such heroism is hardly expected of every artist or even of every leader among artists; but every artist should recognise heroism in others and strive be humble in front of it. Treacherous, disloyal and self-seeking actions are well nigh impossible when people have right ideals to look up to and follow. This is why cultural leaders are so important.

But if an artist is to be a leader and fulfil the role of society's conscience-keeper, it is better to steer clear of official positions in general and the political establishment in particular. Not everybody can be a Victor Hugo, twice elected to power, yet when ideals were betrayed, willing to resign and be banished from France. Pablo Neruda, who represented his country as a diplomat, was equally ready to accept exile. In a somewhat different context Tagore's example springs to mind; though no political radical, the Nobel laureate returned his knighthood subsequent to the massacre at Jallianwalabagh. Such is the stuff that real cultural leaders are made of.

During his 5-year term as a nominated member of Parliament's upper house, the Rajya Sabha, Husain squandered a chance to prove his leadership. He occasionally attended sessions with his sketchbook, producing caricatures unworthy of the name because they were totally devoid of the cutting edge of satire. It would have been much more profitable had he used this time to achieve something that would have benefited all artists as well as the government and ultimately the people of India. Here was a chance to lobby for changes in India's fiscal laws that would aid the conservation of the country's heritage and encourage the growth of a genuine art market, as opposed to the artificial market that now exists.

However, Husain's acts of omission as a Member of Parliament appear insignificant compared to his acts of commission in the face of Hindu fanaticism. The attacks on him a few years ago by the VHP, the Bajrang Dal and others were unequivocally barbaric; nothing can justify vandalism or issuing dire threats to an artist or anyone else. But this barbarism does not put Husain in the right, as most of his fellow artists asserted he was when they took to the streets on his behalf.

Husain's offence is not the fact of his having portrayed Hindu deities in the nude. Everybody slightly educated knows, even some of the Hindu nationalist leaders know, that Hindu deities have been portrayed in their voluptuous glory from the earliest times. Why then the reaction? In part this was because Husain is Muslim, which automatically means that they had been waiting in the wings to wrong foot him. And wrong foot him they did. What had really provoked them was his having taken all kinds of liberties with Hindu subjects while remaining super cautious when dealing with the Islamic. In other words, he played right into their hands.

Having done this, one would have respected him had he stuck to his guns. Instead of recanting as he did, he should have reminded the VHP that for many years he had been selling his paintings based on Hindu themes including some paintings the VHP would probably consider sacrilegious - to the Hindu rich, including Non Resident Indians. The VHP would then have been put in its place for it would have become clear to the world at large that the same individuals who are funding their organisation so generously have also for many years been Husain's patrons and collectors of his Hindu imagery.

But Husain had other plans in mind. At the time of the attacks on him he was already on the way to making his first feature film and nothing was going to stop him. Perhaps he would have apologised whatever his plans, but he might have avoided kowtowing to Bal Thakeray had he not so desperately needed the Shiv Sena supremo's blessings.

There are some who would say that he did the right thing for *Gaja Gamini* turned out to be a very well made film. It is rhythmically paced and visually superb so that the audience is held from beginning to end. Husain's framing and use of colour and light showed him to have a real feeling for the medium; he also succeeded in bringing out the finer qualities in Madhuri Dixit and the rest of his cast. Whether he can sustain the impetus remains to be seen. But on the basis of *Gaja Gamini* alone one can say that he should have become seriously involved in the film medium long ago and left the art world in peace.

Having said this, however, it is difficult to imagine that had Husain not been around to lord over the art world, it would have been a better place. Without him, it would probably have been dominated by somebody equally opportunistic but with less basic talent. In any case, a single artist, no matter how big, does not an art world make.

It is not on account of a dearth of talent that Indian mainstream contemporary art presents an overall picture of utter mediocrity. There are a number of artists - like Husain - who did good work in the past, but having established their styles like brand names, are repeating themselves to death, thereby surrendering to the demands of patronage. There are many others who show signs of promise but these are rarely fulfilled because these artists, too, succumb to the lures of the so-called market, chasing quick success.

It would be only too easy to blame unenlightened patronage, an unregulated market and a decadent environment for the withering of so much talent. But this would tantamount to admitting that artists are robots with no say in the matter, which clearly is not the case. If the artist claims freedom - as he or she must in order to create - then responsibility is implied. Nobody is free, whether an artist or not, once they enter the stage where all the world walks. As soon as that happens one becomes a social being, responsible for others as they are for us. In this sense there are constraints on freedom.

By claiming a professional freedom most others are denied, the artist has a special responsibility. And the basis of this is his professional integrity. Before anything else, artists have to develop and preserve their talents. This involves understanding and building upon their strengths, working on their weaknesses, acquiring ever greater mastery of their medium. With this kind of commitment all else follows:

greater clarity of thought and vision leading to an increased capacity to communicate ideas and feelings to others. And when this happens it becomes much more difficult for the artist to compromise standards; instead it will make him stand tall as a professional and as a human being.

The role of the artist as a social being, a communicator, does not demand activism in art itself. If an artist wants to help change the world, social or political activism is the right path, and his skill may sometimes be exploited to this end. He may, for example, design posters or illustrate pamphlets carrying a message. But when it comes to art, his freedom cannot be harnessed. As Ernst Fischer says:

> The social responsibility of the artist cannot mean that... he writes, paints or composes as so-and-so decrees. But it does mean that instead of working in a vacuum, he recognises that he is ultimately commissioned by society... He produces for a community... The desirable synthesis (is) freedom of the artist's personality in harmony with the collective.

Talk of the collective is romantic in our times, when society is becoming more and more fragmented. But dreams are necessary, and one of the artist's chief roles is to keep them alive. To fulfil this demands many qualities: sincerity and clarity of purpose; the courage and endurance to swim against the tides of perverse fashion; the strength to face personal failure, yet keep persevering. All these things, much more than talent, are the essential constituents of art - good or great. And, as implied by George Eliot, they also form the backbone of genius. As she says:

> Genius at first is little more than a great capacity for receiving discipline.

Receiving discipline means practising self-discipline, not having it forced upon one. Genius or not, every truly creative individual - artist or scientist - needs self-discipline because, in the end, it is liberating. The control or mastery one acquires from it gives one the freedom to think and accomplish creatively.

Often, the artists who talk loudest about freedom are the most illiberal when it comes to the work of artists that does not conform to their own ideology or agenda. And among the biggest culprits here are the 'leftists' and 'left-leaning liberals'.

Most in the art world of this persuasion seek to prove their moral and intellectual superiority by projecting a socially oriented art that is founded on theories so complex as to require volumes of explanation. So when an artist presents work that does not fit this agenda, when the work is so lucid it needs few or no words, the 'leftists' and 'liberals' turn away, don their blinkers and close the gallery doors.

This is an insidious form of dictatorship, and it is very effective because they form powerful cliques and cabals. And when they come together, they form a formidable front that many artists cannot resist. Indeed, they have sucked more artists into their fold than any other power group.

The sad part of it is that the cause they have come to represent over the past years is a right one. The struggle for maintenance of communal harmony and resistance against retrogressive political and religious forces is necessary and just. But those engaged in the struggle would do well to ask themselves why they have so far achieved so little in stemming those forces. Had they been more effective in confronting them, the gruesome events of 2002 in Gujarat might have been avoided.

It is a struggle that has been waged since 1984 and the anti-Sikh pogroms ensuing from Indira Gandhi's assassination. Eight years later this gathered momentum with the destruction of Babur's Mosque and the resultant communal riots. That the experience of these events did not spur the liberal-left and secular forces towards self-introspection, a rethinking of strategy and structuring, is but a symptom of their undemocratic mindset and manner of functioning. And any organisation or group that thinks and functions in an undemocratic way is the enemy of freedom.

Specifically with respect to the artists associated with this group, there is a prevailing belief that fascist and fundamentalist forces can be resisted through works of art. In today's India - where the masses' minds are enslaved by popular films and television entertainment - this is a highly romantic notion to say the least. People do need art to give them courage and hope in their struggle for justice and peace, but the days are gone when paintings like David's could unite people against oppression. Besides, David was a genuine revolutionary, which today's artists and intellectuals most certainly are not.

Society's conscience keepers do not uphold the revolutionary principles of liberty, equality and fraternity by paying lip service to them in their art and art related activities. In order to exorcise evil, the visionary sorcerer has to begin by being true to himself in his art and in his life. Thereafter, the means he adopts will be dependent on his gifts, temperament, experience and socio-political circumstances. But whatever means he chooses, a degree of sacrifice will be demanded of him. As underlined when talking of Courbet, principles can never be upheld without some form of sacrifice. At present in India, as in most of the world, leftist-liberal artists and intellectuals want the best of both worlds. They want to be seen the forefront of pro-people movements without conceding a single inch of their privileged territories. Under such circumstances it is hardly surprising that rightwing forces are rising triumphant.

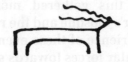

There was a time not so long ago when Indian artists, fired by the spirit of the freedom movement, were working to evolve a modern language rooted in Indian tradition, yet inspired by the winds of change blowing across the world.

The largest number of such artists emanated from Bengal. This was in large part due to the cohesiveness given to the movement by Tagore through the foundation of his university at Shantiniketan. Spanning several generations, his nephews Abanindranath and Gaganendrath, Nandalal Bose, Benod Behari Mukherjee and Ramkinkar were among the many talents to produce a body of work of outstanding quality in a wide variety of media, subjects and styles. Jamini Roy, Chittaprasad, Gobardan Ash, Gopal Ghosh and Sailoz Mukherjea join the roll call of Bengali artists whose work remained firmly rooted in the Indian soil and in the soul of its people. And through their art, the dignity of the people was restored after a gap of three centuries or more.

Among other names that must be remembered in the same light is Amrita Shergil. Even though her work reflects a deep melancholy that is uncharacteristic of the Indian people, she achieved at a young age a synthesis of Indian tradition and European modern art that paved a road for future generations. Just after Independence this road was initially taken by the Progressives of Bombay, among them Francis Newton Souza, S. H. Raza and M.F. Husain. The early work of all these artists, Souza's Goan subjects in particular,

Plate 1

After You!, Honoré Daumier

Plate 2 *Mara's Assault*, Sanchi

Plate 3 *There is a lot to suck*
Francisco Goya

Plate 4

Guernica (detail), Pablo Picasso

Plate 5

The White General
George Grosz

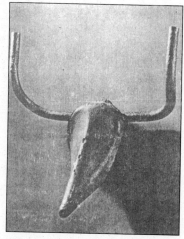

Plate 6

Bull's head
Pablo Picasso

Plate 7   *Head of a Nobleman*, Mathura

Plate 8   *David* (detail), Michelangelo

Plate 9   *Dancing Wizards*, Bhimbetka

Plate 10   *Mummers disguised as animals*, Flemish

Plate 11   *Dukhopadana Jataka*, Mathura

Plate 12   *Starving Peasants*, Chittaprasad

Plate 21   *Nymph and Rishyashring*, Mathura

Plate 22   *Egg Rise*, Anil Karanjai

Plate 23

The Floating Conch, Hieronymus Bosch

Plate 24

Shiva's snake deserts him, Pahari

Plate 25   *A Nobleman*, Gaganendranath Tagore

Plate 26   *Triumvirate of Evil*, Suraj Ghai

Plate 27   *The Dying Princess*, Ajanta

Plate 28   *Boddhisattva Padmapani*
(detail) Ajanta

pointed towards a still more brilliant future. But the group's unity was short-lived. While Souza and Raza established themselves in England and France respectively, Husain became the darling of the establishment at home. And so began the squandering of their talents. The only member of the Progressives to remain on course was K.H. Ara. Although Ara's work was often randomly produced, it was always firmly implanted in the ethos of Bombay - the people's Bombay - which was as familiar to him as the back of his hand.

If there is any redemption for Indian contemporary art, there has to be a return to and reassessment of these promising beginnings. No less essential is the identification and appraisal of those few artists who have carried the torch against impossible odds. Artists who have not betrayed their role as society's conscience keepers by succumbing to the temptation of easy success, of incorporation into a rotten establishment. Artists who have sided with the forces of change. Artists who have remained committed to developing a language that has meaning for a larger society and continues to uphold the dignity and ideals of the people, their hopes for a better life. Artists who have analysed the world like scientists in order to demystify it and inspire others with their knowledge and clarity of vision.

PART II

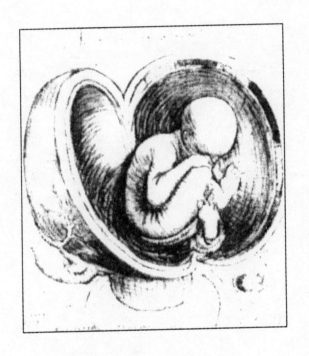

ART AND SCIENCE

When it comes to atoms, language can be used only as in poetry. The poet, too, is not nearly so concerned with describing facts as with creating images.

Niels Bohr
Danish physicist

The popular belief that art and science belong to separate spheres of human activity is a product of our specialised, fragmented times. Right from our childhood most of us have been brought up with the idea that if we have a bent for anything it must be either for science *or* art. We are also taught to think that a genius like Leonardo da Vinci was merely 'a Renaissance man', as though an artist-scientist could only have happened in the Europe of that age. In truth, as we shall see, to be any good at all, an artist always has a scientific mind, just as a scientist always thinks creatively.

Another common misconception is that the arts have flourished only when science has floundered and vice versa. Many even believe that science is a destroyer of culture, a thesis squarely contradicted by history. In *The Common Sense of Science*, an indignant Jacob Bronowski asks:

> What is this golden age of art untarnished by the breath of crude mechanics? Where did it exist? In the East? The civilisations of Egypt, of India, and of the Arabs belie it... In the West? The culture of the West begins in Greece; and in the great age of Greece, art and science penetrate one another more closely than in any modern age.

Bronowski also challenges the notion that a layperson is unable to appreciate science:

Many people… cheerfully write off the large intellectual pleasures of science as if they belonged only to minds of a special cast. Science…is as wide as the literal meaning of its name: knowledge. The notion of the specialised mind is by comparison as modern as the specialised man, "the scientist", a word which is only a hundred years old.

A similar attitude has developed towards art, and here the reference is to visual art as opposed to the arts in general. Many people equally write off the pleasures of seeing, ignoring the importance of visual knowledge and the visual experience, as if only specialists had eyes. And, like science, art is as wide as its literal meaning: creative skill.

The layperson's resistance to scientific investigation cannot in the main be blamed on scientists. The fault lies with the system educational and economic which imposes specialisation on society. Besides, in more recent times the mass media and scientists have joined forces to change the old mindset. Television channels like Discovery and National Geographic have achieved a great deal in popularising science, including complex areas like quantum physics and genetics.

Art is unpopular, on the other hand, because it has been mystified by artists and others of the field, namely art historians and critics. Exceptions can be cited in personalities like Kenneth Clark and John Berger whose BBC series, respectively *Civilisation* and *Ways of Seeing*, had an immense public following. Thanks to Berger's down to earth, iconoclastic approach, this was especially true of *Ways of Seeing*. But in the three decades since it was broadcast, television programmes on art have on the whole remained conservative and dull. As a result, public interest in the subject has again dwindled.

Yet art history is a social science and ought to be an invaluable educational tool. When properly told, the story of art and artists is the story of a people. And it enjoys the advantage of dealing with images which serve, literally, to open people's eyes onto the past.

In India, television has failed entirely to create a viewership for art programmes because the approach of producers and directors has been pedantic and narrow. There has been a marked tendency to compartmentalise the subject which is boring as well as misleading. For example, the national channel, Doordarshan has telecast at least two series on 'the history of Indian painting' as though this discipline evolved in isolation from sculpture. Moreover, the concept of Indian art history as a social science does not yet appear to have taken root among experts of the subject.

As to contemporary art, most of it leaves the layperson utterly bewildered. And one of the main reasons behind this is political: artists and their cohorts have a vested interest in remaining inaccessible to a larger public; this is the only way they can get away with what they do. Another reason is the want of scientific thinking among them.

Today's artists have lost sight of the fact that one side of their creativity involves science. It is not merely that artworks are material entities demanding technical skill and knowledge in their execution; they are also expressions of ideas, experiences and feelings which, although personal, have a base in the society to which the artist belongs. Aesthetics is a scientific subject that reflects the overall development of a society. This means that a knowledge of aesthetics in historical perspective is essential to the artist if he or she is to produce anything worthwhile.

Consciousness of the inextricable relationship between art and science is much higher among scientists than among artists. This is particularly true of those involved in abstract fields like physics and mathematics. Indeed, many of these have talked about their creative experiences when working on or discovering theories and formulae.

Insights into these experiences are discussed in a paper entitled, *The Science Of Beauty, The Art Of Thrill* by N. Mukunda of the Indian Institute of Science, Bangalore. Written in a language accessible to the layperson, Mukunda's paper begins by quoting renowned scientists on the subject of beauty and harmony in mathematics and physics, the discovery of which is often deeply thrilling. For instance, he recalls Einstein's statement about the 'magic' inherent the theory of general relativity. He also cites Werner Heisenberg, best known for the Uncertainty Principle, which has played such an important role in the development of both quantum mechanics and modern philosophy. In 1925, two years prior to the evolution of this formula, Heisenberg had developed the theory of quantum mechanics called matrix mechanics. Much later he described his feeling of deep alarm at the moment of discovery; he talked of

> the strangely beautiful interior (perceived)
> through the surface of atomic phenomena

and he recalls feeling giddy when he confronted the wealth of mathematical structures laid out for him by nature.

Mukunda observes that the kind of emotions felt by Einstein, Heisenberg and other discoverers

> must be very close to those of great artists at
> the moments of their best creations.

Here Mukunda makes a very valid point, but by failing to explain it, he draws a veil of mystery over it. We need to ask in concrete terms what is felt by a true artist, great or not, at a highly creative moment. And how does this meet the scientist's experience?

To answer these questions one must first consider the commonness of the basic aims and processes of the artist and scientist. Both attempt to fathom the world so as to create order out of the world's chaos and to share their knowledge and experience of it with others. Both begin with an idea or an abstract concept, which they set out to prove or make concrete through the material and knowledge at their disposal and through technical skill. And both inscribe their work with a signature or QED when that idea or concept has been structured as perfectly as possible.

Another meeting point between the two is visualisation. This becomes clear when one recalls Heisenberg's statement on the perception of beauty in his formula. His words are echoed by his colleague Niels Bohr who observed that, like the poet, the atomic physicist is concerned with creating images.

But an artwork and an equation or theory differ radically in that the former becomes an immediately concrete object or entity while the latter remains an abstraction to be applied. The moment a temple sculpture was finished, it was there to be seen and appreciated; when Beethoven completed a symphonic score, it was there to be played; Shakespeare wrote his dramas for immediate performance. But when Archimedes or Newton put his name to his discovery, it remained a theoretic formula. In this sense, the artist's emotions in the face of a finished work are probably touched more by joy than the scientist's. The artist's creative processes seem to lead to a more complete objective experience.

There are other major differences between their work: whereas the scientist strives to discover laws or concepts that are universally valid, the artist strives to adapt existing laws to express a personal understanding; and whereas a scientific law can be invalidated by subsequent discoveries, a work of art has permanent validity because it represents a particular culture at a particular moment in history.

In the second part of his paper Mukunda draws further comparisons between the two fields of creativity. His argument is largely based on the observations of two distinguished scientists: the physicist, S. Chandrashekhar and the molecular geneticist Gunther Stent. Citing the essay of the former on Shakespeare, Newton and Beethoven, he points out that the life pattern of the scientist often differs radically from that of the artist. While the scientist tends to an enormous burst of creative activity in a short time span, the artist tends to work in a continuum, generally producing his best works towards the end of his life.

In putting forward possible reasons for this, Mukunda cites the distinguished mathematician, Harish Chandra. Chandra feels that scientific advances may demand the daring of the young mind, its imagination not inhibited by a surfeit of knowledge, whereas artistic achievement is more the product of experience and emotional development. This is a very valuable insight for young artists and writers who almost invariably strive to prove their uniqueness, their greatness, before they have begun to be sufficiently competent.

Stent argues that within every true scientist exists an artist and that every true artist is also a scientist. He rejects the prevailing view that an artistic creation is unique and his logic is based on the example of Shakespeare. He correctly suggests that much of the Bard's material - his ideas, plots and characters - were drawn from the classics and other earlier sources. So his uniqueness lies only in what he made of this material. In other words, his starting point was knowledge or science and this he expressed through his own experience and emotions to bring forth works of art.

Stent also believes that the difference between the artist's and scientist's process is superficial. Here his logic is based on the example of Watson and Crick, the discoverers of the DNA double helix structure. Crick himself said that had he and his partner not succeeded, the discovery would have been made by others within no more than a few years.

Stent counters with the observation that even if this were the case, it is most unlikely that the discovery would have been made in exactly the same way. In other words, *how* a scientist expresses a solution is based on his individual emotional make-up and experience rather than on classical knowledge. In this way scientific discoveries become works of art.

With respect to the layperson's understanding of this phenomenon, Bronowski asserts:

> The layman's key to science is in its unity with the arts. He will understand science as a culture when he tries to trace it in his own culture.

One can reply that the reverse is equally true. If science cannot be properly approached and understood without placing it in the light of art and culture, then the layperson needs to approach art in the light of science. In fact, for reasons already noted, this way round it is all the more necessary.

In an Indian context, Bronowski's emphasis on tracing science in one's own culture is particularly important because the prevailing view among Indians is that science is a western phenomenon. For the westernised elite that rules the country the concept of an indigenous science barely exists. Where it does exist it is generally believed to belong firmly to the past.

The notion that Indian science cannot be modern or modernised is paralleled in art. Indian art traditions are thought of either as static or as entities to be made contemporary only when translated into a western language. The irrationality of this view will soon be laid bare.

In his illuminating essay, *Indian Cultural Manifestations and the West*, Amartya Sen cites the observations of two thinkers of the past on the subject of India's contribution to world culture. The first of them is al-Sabhadi, a medieval poet of Baghdad, who recorded that in his day there were three things in which the Indian nation prided itself: its method of reckoning, the game of chess and the book titled Kalila Wa Dimna, a collection of legends and fables.

The second of those quoted is none other than the giant Voltaire, doyen of the Age of Enlightenment. Through him it is revealed that in 18th century Europe India was recognised for the very same achievements and more. Voltaire acknowledges France's debt to India in

> our numbers, our backgammon, our chess, our
> first principles of geometry and the fabies
> which have become our own.

Yet, as Sen underlines, such a selection of achievements would fit neither the general western image of India today nor the way many Indians perceive themselves and their intellectual past. Some awareness of this country's mathematical prowess does of course exist, but not many acknowledge that without Indian numerals and the decimal system, the west could never have lead the world in science and technology. As pointed out by A.L. Basham in *The Wonder That Was India*:

> Most of the great discoveries and inventions of
> which Europe is so proud would have been
> impossible...if Europe had been shackled by
> the unwieldy system of Roman numerals.

As an aside, Basham also underlines the well known fact that it was the Greeks, not the Indians, whose mathematical science was based on geometry. Indian mathematical thinking was abstract and this led to the rudimentary algebra carried to Europe by the Arabs. So what Voltaire must have meant was that the France's first principles of algebra were the gift of India.

But if India's mathematical contribution to the world has been misunderstood or underplayed, its contribution to western medicine has been sorely neglected. It is true that the international interest in Ayurveda has been growing by leaps and bounds, but this has not lead to a proper assessment of the subject. Ayurvedic medicine is perceived by most as a range of 'herbal' remedies rather than as a scientific system with an underlying philosophy and a long history. In fact, in therapeutics probably no other ancient culture was so advanced or famous as India. Greek physicians were known to have travelled here to study the subject. Where India lagged behind Greece was mainly in anatomy, a branch of medicine severely frowned upon by the Brahman orthodoxy.

In *Science and Society in Ancient India*, Debiprasad Chattopadhyaya cites a body of evidence to prove that the Indian physicians were far from being purveyors of mumbo-jumbo and had evolved a system in many respects similar to the Hippocratic and in some respects in advance of it. He asserts that

> In ancient India, the only discipline that promises to be fully secular and contains clear potentials of the modern understanding of natural science is medicine... (It took) the momentous step from magico-religious therapeutics to rational therapeutics.

Chattopadhyaya further affirms that this step was fully understood by the physicians and incorporated into their terminology. Referring to key texts they compiled, he notes:

> Discarding scripture-orientation, they insist on the supreme importance of direct observation of natural phenomena and on...a

81

rational processing of the empirical data. They even (claim) that the truth of any conclusion…is to be tested ultimately by the criterion of practice.

That this historical knowledge has been overlooked or underplayed and that many Indians have lost sight of their intellectual heritage is, according to Amartya Sen, the outcome of

> …the selective alienation of India from…the rationalist part of its tradition.

Sen believes that this has been nourished by

> …the asymmetric relation between India and the West.

But whatever the reasons for it, the alienation has led to an undesirable emphasis on the metaphysical and exotic aspects of tradition. Sen does not deny the importance of mysticism and religious initiatives, but what he does deplore is the picture of India historically starved of intellectual pursuits and overwhelmed by religious preoccupations.

Perhaps strangely, it is not only the Hindu right that projects this picture. Many liberal and leftist intellectuals also give it credence, presumably because they believe it or because they have neither the knowledge nor inclination to challenge it. It is surely ironic that almost the only voices to laud India's past achievements are those subscribing to a narrow nationalist ideology which attributes those achievements to religion. This reinforces the perception of an unscientific and obscurantist culture.

Of all the civilisations of the ancient world, none developed a science of aesthetics as ingenious and comprehensive as the Indian. Not even the Greeks with their Aristotle surpassed India in this field. This is not to deny the many meeting points of the Indian and Greek aestheticians. As already noted with respect to medicine, ties between the two cultures were strong. And in Indian art and drama there are many traces of Greek influence. In the main, however, as a consequence of colonial history, experts have grossly overestimated the Greek influence on Indian art. Splendid as the best of it is, classical Greek and Greco-Roman art can never approximate the best of Indian classical art for expressiveness, above all for its sensuous and subliminal qualities. In general, moreover, Indian aesthetic principles are so different from the Greek that any possible comparisons between the two must be regarded as superficial.

Yet if asked to explain in a few words what is understood by 'aesthetics', most people everywhere would probably come up with an answer close to Aristotle's: this ancient Greek philosopher defined aesthetics as that which concerns itself with the nature of beauty.

Although this classic definition is still valid, it remains inadequate because it immediately demands another definition - that of beauty - and this leads one too soon into another discussion. What is required instead is a modern, much more comprehensive interpretation of the term 'aesthetics', which derives from the Greek *aesthesis*, literally sensory perception. The Russian aesthetician, Yuri Borev provides just such an interpretation. In *Aesthetics: A Textbook* he states:

> Aesthetics is that branch of knowledge which deals with the historically determined essence of human values, their creation, perception, appreciation and assimilation. It is a philosophical science...concerned with the laws of the beautiful.

What may first strike one about this definition is that it closely corresponds to the contents and approach of key ancient Indian texts on the subject. The two texts that immediately come to mind are the *Natyashastra* (circa 2nd century), Bharata's famous treatise on drama and dance, and the lesser known *Vishnudharmottara* (circa 4th-7th century), by an unknown author or authors, which deals with the visual arts or 'image-making'. Neither of these texts defines aesthetics as such but there is an underlying assumption that they are concerned with both philosophy and science. Moreover, both of them deal with every aspect of the subject cited by Borev.

The alienation of Indians from this knowledge is in large part responsible for the erroneous perception that Indian art had no rational base and that it fulfilled only a religious demand. It is of course true that most surviving ancient Indian art belongs to sacred monuments. But this does not mean that the same artists never put their minds and hands to use for works of a temporal character. Equally, it does not indicate that those who created sacred art did so in a trance or a frenzy of religious fervour and that there was little or no intellect guiding them. Such absurd assumptions have their roots in the era of colonial rule when art became a weapon to justify that rule. Their origins apart, these assumptions are belied by all the available evidence.

One part of the evidence is the art itself. If one knows anything at all about artistic processes and the difficulties involved, and if one looks at some of the finest Indian artworks then one can soon understand that they could never have been achieved unless feeling was matched with as large a measure of rational thought.

As to the dearth of artworks of a secular character, this is because these were generally executed in perishable materials: in the case of sculpture this was mainly wood; paintings were executed on cloth or wooden walls; even paintings executed on a stone surface, like the Ajanta murals, were not very durable, which is why we are left with so few examples. As an additional observation, there are many surviving Indian sculptures which were probably of secular intent. It is known, for instance, that the Kushana emperors, influenced by the Romans, commissioned a large number of portrait statues.

Literary evidence from early Buddhist times forward also attests to the existence of a strong secular tradition. For example, the *Maha Ummaga Jataka* describes the Bodhisattva's great hall and subterranean palace adorned with mural paintings depicting magnificent imaginary landscapes. In the *Vinaya*, reference is made to the King of Kosala's picture gallery which was located in his pleasure grove and visited by many members of the public, including monks. Many later texts, including Kalidas's *Shakuntala*, talk of the many portraits painted by artists of the royal and servant class alike.

The section of the *Vishnudharmottara* devoted to painting confirms the strength of the secular tradition. In the words of its translator, Stella Kramrisch:

> It deals not only with its religious aspect but also, and to a far greater extent, with its secular employment. It proclaims the joy that colours and forms and the representation of things seen and imagined produce. Speaking of artistic representation in relation to religion, it points out their mutual limitations...

The same text also confirms that artistic practice in ancient India was pursued in a rational manner and that an intellectual propensity was needed by the artist as much as skill:

> A painting drawn with care, pleasing to the eye, thought out with supreme intelligence and remarkable by its execution... yields the desired pleasure.

None of this is to suggest that every ancient Indian artist was a genius or towering intellect. In any case, genius in ancient times was more of a collective than individual phenomenon. Works were executed by guilds consisting of masters and apprentices; the masters needed knowledge, experience, a fine hand, and the ability to be a guiding light. For the average good work this was enough. In any culture, great works come only once in a while and to achieve them the artist is driven by forces that are not easily explicable. As Coomaraswamy puts it in *The Arts and Crafts of India and Ceylon*:

> ...great art results from the impulse to express certain clear intuitions of life and death, rather than the conscious wish to make beautiful pictures or songs. The absence of beauty from art, or happiness from life, is an unanswerable condemnation of any civilization in which they are lacking; yet neither beauty nor happiness is easily attainable if sought for a primary end. Very often, as in India, they appear like angels unawares, just where the seeming rigidity of hieratic laws would appear to deny all personal freedom.

On the subject of laws, we should now take a general look at the business of 'image-making' as expounded in the *Vishnudharmottara*. The first thing worth noting is the text's emphasis on mathematics which, being concerned with proportion and harmony, is a very important part of the 'laws of the beautiful'. Rules are laid down for the representation of figures: for every part of the body, from temple to toenail, precise measurements are given for the attainment of a perfectly proportioned figure; five types of male and female figures are defined, each of different size though all of equal proportions.

The text further decrees that in all figures the length of the body must be equal to its breadth from the tips of the middle finger when the arms are outstretched. Today this might appear as a simple calculation that anyone might work out for himself. But if it were really so obvious we should ask ourselves why, around a thousand years later, Leonardo should spend time calculating the very same thing, as illustrated in his famous drawing of a naked male within a square and a circle.

Speaking of which, one cannot find an example of a great Indian artwork that has been composed in the absence of principles based on the square, circle and other geometric forms. As already noted, Indian mathematics was not much concerned with geometry. But as Basham suggests, a simple geometric system evolved here very early probably because, in Vedic times, sacrifice sites had to be laid out with great accuracy.

A sense of geometric harmony among the Indian people evidently existed far further back than the age of the Vedas. For instance, if we look carefully at the superb rock painting called *Dancing Wizards* (plate 9) we can see in our mind's eye that the figures are composed with an almost perfect square and circle. When one considers that this painting belongs to the Middle Stone Age and is possibly as much as 10,000 years old, then one cannot but marvel at its harmonious composition, to say nothing of its other qualities that are elsewhere discussed.

Returning to the *Vishnudharmottara*, the text also places emphasis on the complex laws of foreshortening. For those unfamiliar with the term, this means the method by which figures are composed and proportioned in a spatial composition which recedes towards the horizon. Foreshortening was first put into practice in European painting during the Renaissance, and it is only one step away from perspective.

In the murals at Ajanta one can see examples of foreshortening as well as a sophisticated method of spatial composition. Most of the Ajanta paintings form part of a narrative; space is arranged so that the eye rolls from one part of the story to the next. It is rather like looking through the lens of a slowly panning camera. The eye is not disturbed by elements external to the particular episode one is viewing.

Despite its poor state of conservation, Ajanta gives an idea of the wide palette used by ancient Indian artists. The *Vishnudharmottara* and other sources set out lists of substances from which colour could be obtained: among these was red lead, orpiment, conch shell, soot, sulphuretted arsenic, myrobalan, lac, vermilion, indigo, gold, silver, copper and mica. Elaborate instructions are given for the preparation of colours, the priming of the surfaces to be painted, and the method of colour application. The primary colours are listed, with hundreds of intermediary colours or tones obtained from mixing. But the artist is urged to mix colours

> according to his own logic and imagination, to
> make a thousandfold what is a hundredfold.

The rules regarding colour applied as much to sculpture as to painting. Like all ancient sculpture everywhere in the world, ancient Indian carvings were painted, a rather horrifying thought for most people. Accustomed to admiring the subtle colours and textures of stone, the idea of painted sculpture conjures up gaudily finished images in the mind's eye. But in reality, as the text makes clear, colour was used with discernment and logic. In the hands of a master it must have greatly enhanced the beauty of fine carving.

Just as the sculptor was required to apply colour to his creations, so the painter had to produce the effects of sculpture in his. Painted images had to be three-dimensional. This is why great stress is placed on modelling or shading, without which an image remains flat. As the text says:

> A painting in which an object is devoid of shading is called mediocre.

Just as today, images were modelled through tones of colour and different kinds of lines and brushstrokes; these are specified in detail by the text.

For modelling, as for all other aspects of image-making, the text emphasises the importance of the even handling of a painted surface. The authors ordain:

> A picture which in some parts is shaded and in others remains unshaded is bad... Every part of the object represented should agree with the general treatment of the whole.

Around a millennium and a half later, this 'law of the beautiful' was expressed in similar words by Paul Cézanne, known as 'the father of modern art'.

In an attempt to prove that Indian art was inferior to the European there were several arguments put forward by colonial scholars like James Mill and Alexander Cunningham. The first of these arguments, already answered to some extent, was that Indian art, particularly Hindu art, was imaginary, fantastic and devoid of rationality. A second argument was gender oriented: while European art was characterised as masculine, Indian art was deemed feminine and hence inferior.

That Indian art was not naturalistic in the classical Greek sense of the term was yet another argument to its detriment. In the era under discussion, Greco-Roman naturalism was the European ideal and anything that failed to conform to this was adjudged primitive. In colonial eyes one school of Indian art was exceptional: the Greco-Roman Buddhist school of Gandhara. Situated on the north-west frontier, this had reached its peak during the reign of the Kushana emperors, when mercantile and cultural links extended from China to Rome.

Gandhara sculpture was held not only to be the highest aesthetic achievement of ancient India but also to have exerted enormous influence on the whole of Indian art. On both counts the colonisers were spectacularly wrong. Most Gandhara works are either rather crude or mannered and expressionless. A handful of exceptions are very fine indeed, but they lack the sensuous, tactile quality of other Indian sculpture.

That Indian art did not conform to Greek classical naturalism does not mean that the ancient Indian artists desisted from studying the human figure or nature. On the contrary, the observation and mastery of their manifold forms was urged upon them. As the *Vishnudharmottara* underlines:

> The chief (aim) of painting is to produce an exact likeness. Men should be painted according to their country; their colour, dress and appearance should be well observed.

In another place it states:

> An intelligent artist paints what looks probable.

For mastery of the human figure, the artist was enjoined not only to observe life in minute detail, but also to make a careful study of the art of dance. This did not require the artist to articulate figures in the exact poses of a dancer. In fact, none of the nine poses listed in the *Vishnudharmottara* coincides with any of the 101 poses listed in the *Natyashastra*. So, where do the two arts connect? Kramrisch provides a large part of the answer:

> What is meant by the derivation of painting from dancing is the movement in common to both these expressive forms; it asserts itself in purity through dancing, it guides the hand of the artist, who knows how to paint figures, as if breathing, the wind as blowing, the fire as blazing... that is what is expected to be seen in the work of a painter, to make it alive with rhythm and expression.

Movement apart, Indian dance is dramatic and as such it involves gestures and facial expressions. Much of Indian painting and sculpture was also concerned with story telling and it would therefore have been logical for artists to have a grasp of the dancer-actor's conventions in order to communicate their own narrative.

The *Vishnudharmottara* is replete with the most vivid and detailed descriptions of the kinds of figures and subjects that the artists of that time would have been required to paint. Instructions are given for each of these. It says for instance:

> By one who knows painting, the commander of an army should be represented as strong, proud, tall, with fleshy shoulders... big head, powerful chest, prominent nose and broad chin, with eyes raised up towards the sky... (and) soldiers should generally be painted with frowns on their faces... Bards should have a resplendent dress...and the veins on their neck should be shown. Heralds should

be drawn tawny and squint-eyed... The doorkeeper holds a staff in his hand, does not look very mild... Musicians, dancers and those who can correctly regulate the sound of musical instruments should wear a gorgeous dress... The most respectable people of country and town should be painted with almost grey hair, adorned with ornaments suitable to their rank, wearing white garments, stooping forwards, ready to help and with mien calm by nature. Artisans should be represented eager in the pursuit of their respective crafts. Wrestlers should be drawn with broad shoulders, fleshy limbs, thick neck, head and lips, with closely cropped hair, arrogant and impetuous.

The text lists the appropriate skin colour for the various peoples and social groups of the sub-continent, as well as for foreigners with whom India had contact. It says, for example, that Himalayan people, Greeks and Scyths should be fair, while people from the Deccan and the east coast should be predominantly dark and Brahmans the colour of the moon. Six types of hair are also classified.

Probably the most curious of instructions contained in the *Vishnudharmottara* are those referring to the natural forms or characteristics to be employed in the representation of the human figure. Among are other things we learn that great gods and kings should have snake-like arms and swan-like movements, that the eyes should be shaped like fish when representing lovers, like the petals of a blue lotus in a figure with calm expression and like the petals of a white lotus in a figure expressing fear or grief.

We can be sure these instructions should not be taken too literally for the text later states that everything in it is only a suggestion. Besides, we can see from surviving artworks that the reference is to the essence of a quality in a natural form: the suppleness of a snake, the grace of a swan and so forth. The real point is that a fundamental requirement for the artist was a truly intimate knowledge of nature, a knowledge to be cultivated through constant observation.

Many centuries later, the same became essential for the European artist. Nature studies and still life formed an important part of his oeuvre. Leonardo is a sterling example of a naturalist-artist, and it is no coincidence that of all the European masters prior to the coming of modern art, Leonardo is the closest to Indian art (plates 17 & 18).

We must consider it a tragedy that no secular painting has survived from the ancient era because the *Vishnudharmottara* gives evidence of an immensely rich tradition. We have already seen glimpses of this in the passages cited above.

These passages indicate that the Indian secular tradition would have been unsurpassed in world art before the 16th century when Flemish masters like Pieter Breughel and his sons painted sweeping landscapes with people engaged in all manner of activity, often in a fantastic and satirical vein. A look at more of the guidelines contained in the *Vishnudharmottara* will convince even the sceptical that the ancient Indian masters approached Breughel in variety and even wit. It says, for instance:

> Those engaged in gambling should be drawn devoid of upper garments, the winners merry and the losers full of grief. The battlefield has to be show as containing four divisions... with soldiers engaged in fighting, strewn with corpses and besmeared with blood... The night should be shown with moon, planets and stars, with approaching thieves and men fast asleep and others engaged in worldly

pleasures… women are to be shown going out to meet their lovers… The evening is to be shown by its red glow and by Brahmins engaged in controlling their senses…

As to the way the seasons were to be painted:

(An artist) should represent spring with merry men and women, by "laughing" vernal trees, with bees swarming about and cuckoos. The summer has to be shown with dried pools…languid men…deer seeking the shade…and buffaloes burying themselves in mud… the rainy season by flashes of lightning, beautified by rainbows…heavily laden clouds, birds perched on trees, and lions and tigers sheltered in caves… the autumn with trees heavy with fruits…ripe corn and with tanks beautified by lotuses and swans… the winter with the horizon shrouded in hoar-frost, with shivering men and delighted crows and elephants.

Bearing all this in mind one could say that realism rather than naturalism was the goal of Indian art. Probably one can call it 'magical realism'; often these descriptions of people and nature resonate with the spirit of the great modern Columbian writer, Gabriel García Marquez.

Texts of course remain theoretical, but if proof is needed that Indian painting was deeply rooted in everyday life and occupied such a broad canvas, then we can find this in the Ajanta murals. These also prove that figures in Indian art were modelled on real flesh and blood people. Among the hundreds of figures still discernible, there is a wonderful diversity and individuality. In the finest of them, the essence of the human form is captured with great realism and expressiveness. This is particularly true of the female form.

For instance, the painting titled *The Dying Princess* (plate 27) is one of the most magnificent renderings of the female nude in the history of world art. The drama of the work is intensified by the contradiction between her sensuality and the tragedy of her impending death.

The laws drawn up for the creation of the beautiful were in some ways very strict, but great art has never been a product of rigidity. Those who compiled the *Vishnudharmottara* were fully aware of the importance of creative freedom and so they urged artists to apply their own intellect to their creations. As the text stresses:

> In this treatise only suggestions are given, for
> the subject can never be described in detail
> even in many hundred years.

One cannot but marvel at the farsightedness of the person or persons who compiled this treatise. Could they have had any idea of how valuable it would be at the turn of the 3rd millennium?

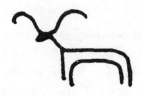

So far, almost everything said about the rational basis of Indian art in antiquity has pertained to the means of creation. A good deal has also been said about the realism of this art. Both these aspects of the subject are of much more than academic interest. They are also necessary weapons in the battle against wrong perceptions of traditional Indian culture which exist in the minds of most westerners and westernised Indians, and which are projected by politico-cultural organisations like the Viswa Hindu Parishad.

But beyond this, in a contemporary context, their relevance is limited in the sense that they cannot be repeated. Nobody today in his or her right mind can even begin to think of creating art as it was created in the past. To believe otherwise would be to believe, like the Hindu nationalists, that nothing can surpass the achievements of the 'Golden Age' and that only these are worth emulating.

If India's science of aesthetics is to be useful today, the elements which give scope for the broadest contemporary interpretation have to be identified. This means distinguishing the area that corresponds to Borev's definition of aesthetics as highlighted above, principally:

> ...the essence of human values, their creation,
> perception, appreciation and assimilation...

This area is found in the theory or system known as *rasa*.

At the very beginning of his essay on the subject, *The Essence of Indian Art*, B.N. Goswamy evaluates the place of *rasa* in Indian aesthetics. He notes that:

The single most important term that figures in
the formal theory of art developed in India
from very early times is undoubtedly *rasa*.

Given its supreme place in an ancient theory, it perhaps
seems astonishing that *rasa* should fit the modern definition
of aesthetics so well. Even in the matter of terminology the
two meet. As Goswamy states, at one level *rasa* means:

> the…essence of a thing…the best or finest part
> of it…like perfume, which comes from matter
> but is not so easy to describe…

More importantly, *rasa* as an aesthetic system is every bit
concerned with human values. The way these are created,
perceived, appreciated and assimilated has a place of major
importance in the *rasa* theory.

All of this is covered and debated at length in various texts,
beginning with Bharata's *Natyashastra.* In fact, so much
importance was given to the subject of *rasa* by aestheticians
and commentators in ancient and medieval times that the
polemics in its respect continued for about fifteen hundred
years. The *Vishnudharmottara* was written within a few
centuries of Bharata's seminal text, and although it does not
enter the debate, it covers *rasa* from the point of view of the
visual arts and has a few unique things to say about it.

But before anything else, we need to ask what is meant by
the essence of human values. If we start with essence and if
we accept that this means 'the finest part of a thing' then we
can be sure that we mean the best of human values. The
right term for this is ideals. Ideals are the standards or goals
a society aspires to, the models or examples people look up
to and desire to emulate.

So now the question comes: how are these ideals
determined? In one sense, as Borev suggests, it is history
that decides them, which is another way of saying that they
change from age to age. Moreover, since they are

conditioned by the ideas and social norms prevalent in a particular age, the sense in which they change is ideological. Therefore, to a large extent, ideals are determined by politico-economic factors.

To give an example, Martin Luther King became an ideal among American blacks and a minority of whites not because he was a religious man versed in the Bible but because of the poverty of blacks, made possible by their oppression. This may sound obvious, but if we do not keep such examples in mind then we may end up believing that what divides the world is culture and not economic and social justice. The 'clash of civilisations' theory is not only upheld by western imperialists and warmongers but by religious fanatics and racists of all hues. The warped ideals upheld by these power groups need to be constantly challenged.

Even the noblest ideals become ignoble when they have run their course and society demands a change. Take, for instance, the medieval ideals of chivalry and romantic love. In Europe, these took the form of knights in shining armour, damsels in distress, jousting tournaments to win the hand of a lady, fights unto the death to prove a point. Today, only lunatics, sado-masochists or hoodlums would hold such things as ideal. There are a great many practices and beliefs in contemporary India that would have represented the highest ideals in a bygone age. *Sati* is one example. It was quite one thing for the wives of warriors to immolate themselves in the wake of a lost battle in order to escape a fate worse than death. It is quite another for a woman to do the same thing today because tradition says this makes her a goddess. This is a gross manipulation of human values, as is the practice of dowry.

Certain other values are determined more by historical space than time; at one particular historic juncture, a value may be positive in one society and negative in another. Take the freedom of women to express their sexuality and choose their own partners: this would be most desirable in Indian middle class families riddled with hypocrisy and inhibitions; and it would be still more desirable in places where the likes of the Taliban rule; but in western societies which are suffering the consequences of promiscuity, more of it would be nothing short of disastrous.

The aesthetic implications of all this are not as complex as might at first appear. To bring it down to the essence, one of the main roles of art and the artist is to uphold values as long as these are relevant and positive; conversely, when they become outdated and negative, it is given to the artist not only to take on the role of the iconoclast and smash them but also to replace them with positive values pointing to the future. This is why we call art prophetic. And it is one of the important ways in which the artist becomes 'a visionary sorcerer'.

Yet human values are not entirely determined by history. At another level they are timeless and universal. For instance, heroism is always heroism no matter what the historical circumstances in which it is manifested. This is not to contradict what has just been said. It has never been heroic to commit *sati*; while in the past it was honourable, today it is just a tragic waste of life. True heroism may involve both honour and tragedy, but it is something much larger; it means taking action for the greater good of society.

In another vein take humour. Humour is always humour, even if its sources and references differ from culture to culture. The ability to laugh and make laugh is one of the most positive of human ideals, although this does not make it any less corruptible than anything else. The visionary sorcerer can prevent ideals from lapsing into decadence by adapting them to needs of a modern age.

In his study of Indian culture and society, *The Speaking Tree*, Richard Lannoy says:

> The Indian aesthetic sensibility was once the primary means to create a civilization. Some of the most advanced Western thinking of our day is devoted to the problem of reconciling the aesthetic with the scientific, while overcoming the disastrous effects of having allowed bourgeois aesthetic culture to have become implicated in modern fascism. There is every hope that India may play a positive role in this reconciliation... Powerful, immediate sensory images supply the model of relatedness India most urgently needs

Lannoy wrote these words more than thirty years ago, and at that time he could have had no idea of the form modern fascism would take. Nor could he have guessed how much further away Indian art would be led by its practitioners and promoters from playing a reconciliatory role between the aesthetic and the scientific. However, his point still stands. Human and aesthetic values and ideals are thoroughly corruptible.

All of which points us back to *rasa*. If India is to fulfil Lannoy's hope then Indian artists will have to have recourse to *rasa* because the *rasa* theory itself reconciles art and science just as it cries out for development and modernisation.

No discussion on *rasa* can make any sense without first looking at a few definitions. For this purpose, Goswamy's long essay in *The Essence of Indian Art* is a very useful source. The publication is, in fact, the catalogue of an exhibition he curated in which *rasa* was the focus, and it covers nearly every aspect of what seems initially a very complex, sometimes contradictory subject. Even the term itself is at first bewildering when one sees how many senses in which it is used.

As Goswamy says, every Indian knows that the most basic meaning of *rasa* is the juice or sap of plants. His definition in the sense of essence has already been cited, and he notes that in its most widely used aesthetic sense:

> *rasa* denotes taste, flavour, relish often yielding pleasure.

As must be clear, *rasa* here has an abstract as well as physical meaning. The flavour of a poem, painting or piece of music would be an accurate rendering of the term in this sense.

Goswamy further notes that in its subtlest sense, *rasa* means:

> a state of heightened delight…the kind of bliss that can be experienced only by the spirit.

In this light, *rasa* can be defined as a materialist philosophic concept. It encompasses the premise that spiritual fulfilment leads from, and is the highest form of, physical experience.

Goswamy also quotes the dicta of other *rasa* authorities. For Viswanatha, the 14th century author of the *Sahitya Darpana* (literally, mirror of literature), the very existence of poetry depended on *rasa*. He said that

> Poetry is a sentence the soul of which is *rasa*.

And Coomaraswamy called *rasa*

> the delight of reason…

In another place he referred to it as

> ideal beauty…

Lannoy speaks of it as

> emotional resonance... aesthetic rapture...

As if to further underline the complexity of the subject, an abundance of terms derives from *rasa*. A *rasika* is a connoisseur, one whose sensitivity to the arts allows her or him or to taste or experience *rasa*; *rasasvadana*, literally the tasting of flavour, is aesthetic fulfilment; a *rasavat* is a work of art possessing *rasa*, while *rasili* means charged with the same; an imperfect aesthetic experience is called *rasabhasa*, while *nirasa* means without *rasa*.

When talking about the theory in general and its application, Goswamy notes that

> the subject bristles with problems...

He points out that even after a millennium and a half of lively debate, some aspects of the subject remained obscure. In addition, scholars in more recent times have had difficulties - and have created them - in interpreting *rasa* on account of language: different words have been used when translating Sanskrit terms into English.

For example, most scholars refer to *rasa* as 'sentiment'. This is a correct term in the academic sense since sentiment is defined as a mixture of thought and feeling, especially refined or tender feeling; it is also classified as an emotion conveyed in art. However, the word seems somewhat archaic today which the concept of *rasa* is not; also it tends to connote something mawkish or cloying. At the same time, it is difficult to replace it with another term. Some scholars talk of 'flavour', which is certainly more down to earth and contemporary, but it does not quite convey the fullness of the term. 'Feeling' comes close because it connotes emotion, physical sensation and thinking or view, all of which are embraced by *rasa*. But this is perhaps too loose a term for a theoretic concept.

Strangely enough, the sense in which *rasa* means sentiment or flavour is the simplest and most straightforward part of the theory. And because it is fundamental to all Indian art forms, with music as the base, its existence is well known among laypeople. This does not mean that its reiteration is unnecessary.

Most texts on the subject list nine distinct *rasas*, each with its corresponding mood and colour. At the top of the list comes *shringara*, the erotic, associated with romantic love and the colours of night. Next comes *hasya*, the comic, and *karuna*, the pathetic or compassionate; their corresponding colours are respectively white for mirth and grey for sorrow. The sentiments associated with anger and action are *raudra*, the furious and *vira*, the heroic; while the former corresponds to anger and red, the latter corresponds to energy and yellow. These are followed by *bhayanaka*, the terrible and *bibhatsa*, the odious, respectively associated with fear and disgust, black and blue; these are flavours one can associate with today's horror genre. The penultimate rasa is *adbhuta*, the marvellous or astonishing, associated with the supernatural or unknown and the colour of gold. Last but not least comes *shanta*, the quiescent or peaceful, associated with holy places and the colour of jasmine and the moon.

What ought to strike everyone about this list is that it comprises all the basic emotions and ideals with which all of us are familiar - emotions and ideals that our species has experienced or yearned for since we began to walk the earth. One can say, therefore, that the flavours of *rasa* represent the essence of timeless and universal human values.

A possible exception to this is the odious. In the Indian tradition, odious or ugly deities are the destroyers of evil and are hence ideals; the same is true of certain non-European cultures, specially the African, and even in the European tradition the hideous and repugnant have an important place in art. Some people might believe that the terrible is an exception but, in the ideal sense, that which causes fear enters the domain of the sublime. A little later

103

on, each of the nine *rasas* will be discussed in greater detail in order to throw light on them as ideals.

There are two main areas of difficulty in understanding *rasa*. The first arises because, as Coomaraswamy notes, there are two distinct senses in which the word *rasa* is used; on the one hand it relates to the nine *rasas*, already cited, and on the other hand it is used in the singular

> with reference to the interior act of tasting flavour.

The second problem arises from the first, because this raises a huge and much debated question: How does the spectator taste flavour? What is the recipe for a true aesthetic experience?

According to Bharata and other authorities the *rasa* recipe contains several ingredients. The mood (*bhava*) is of primary importance, but it is subject to the determinants *(vibhava)*, which encompass the theme of the work and the environment in which it is set. Then there are the consequents (*anubhava*); these are facial expressions, gestures and poses. Two kinds of emotional states are also essential to the recipe: these are the durable (*sthayibhava*) and transitory (*vyabhicharabhava*) feelings that may arise in a situation or the course of a story.

But even Bharata seems to contradict himself when it comes to the mixing of the ingredients. In one place he says tersely:

> *Rasa* is born out of the union of the determinants, the consequents and the complementary emotional states.

And in another elaborate passage he states:

> ...as taste results from a combination of various spices, vegetables and other articles...so the durable emotional states, when they come together with various other psychological states, attain the quality of a sentiment...

104

Later authorities argued the toss and at the end of the day most seem to have agreed, albeit obliquely, with Bharata's second recipe. According to this, when the ingredients are mixed in the right proportion, a durable emotional state emerges and then transmutes itself into a *rasa* in a sensitive and cultured person, a *rasika*; a spark then leaps from the performance or artwork to the *rasika*, resulting in an experience that infuses her or his entire being. The theoreticians also concluded that the *rasika* may not always taste *rasa* at the same level of intensity on every occasion, and that one *rasika*'s depth of experience may vary from that of another.

There is also a broad consensus among authorities that the *rasa* experience is intellectual as much as emotional. With poetic brilliance, one commentator described the experience as

> a condensed understanding in the mode of ecstasy.

The texts contain long discussions on the many obstacles to tasting *rasa*. But Bharata and later authorities agree that this depends a great deal on the energy that the spectator brings to a work of art. As highlighted by Goswamy:

> The durable emotional state that is subtly brought into being through a work of art is one thing: its transmutation into a *rasa* is dependent upon the energy, the inner ability, the singleness of heart of the *rasika*. The faculty of imagination and wonder is greatly emphasized.

A very fascinating aspect of the centuries long debate on *rasa* is the question of whether an artist may experience it. Viswanatha says that

> he may obtain aesthetic experience from the spectacle of his own performance.

But the experiencing of emotion before or during the act of creation is different from the tasting of *rasa*, which is

> a lightning flash of delight

and can only be experienced by the artist when in the position of a spectator.

In discussions about *rasa*, the theoreticians were careful to make distinctions between art and life, between aesthetic fulfilment and basic emotional or psychological experiences. In other words, it was clear in their minds that in a theatrical performance the *rasika* tastes, for instance, the heroic flavour without actually wanting to kill the villain himself.

When speaking of *rasa* in relation to 'image-making', the *Visnudharmottara* steers clear of polemics and complexities. In listing the nine *rasas* it merely suggests the kind of images suitable for each. Where it makes a unique contribution is in the matter of what kind painting should go where. The text stresses that that only the erotic, comic and quiescent *rasas* are suitable for homes or for the private quarters of the king. It further pleads that all the other *rasas* should be viewed in public places like temples or the quarters of the king's palace occupied by the assembly halls. Among the images forbidden in private homes or quarters are:

> men with ugly features, or those inflicted by sorrow due to death and pity, war and the burning ground...

The authors suggest, on the other hand, that a skilfully executed work in which the mood of love, laughter or peace predominates

> cleanses and curbs anxiety, causes unequalled and pure delight and kills the evils of bad dreams...

This is surely a view with which most modern psychologists would agree.

Although not specifically related to *rasa*, another gem from the authors reads:

> The place where a picture is firmly placed
> does not look empty.

This is a view which all contemporary artists and dealers would not hesitate to endorse.

And finally in the *Visnudharmottara,* a list is drawn up of all the possible defects in an artist's work that make it null and void as art. High on the list is the absence of *rasa*. This is a view with which modern experts of the subject like B.N. Goswamy concur wholeheartedly. As he stresses:

> That *rasa* is what art is all about may not be
> specifically stated...but in a very real sense it
> is what a viewer is looking for in a work of art.

There is no disputing this logic. In front of a painting or sculpture, listening to music or poetry, in a theatre or cinema hall, reading a book, what the spectator is really seeking is the experience of taste or flavour, something which yields pleasure and an emotional charge. The flavour may be sweet, fiery, sour, salty, tangy, pungent, bitter or soothing, but what is desired is the gratification or lifting of the spirit, as well as food for thought. At its very highest, the sought after experience is a flash of realisation matched with a feeling of delight which is almost sexual in its intensity. The tasting of *rasa* both enlightens and enraptures the *rasika*.

Of course, when the taste buds of the spectator are underdeveloped or corrupted, fine flavouring will not yield the desired experience. But when her or his palate is sensitive, then the subtlest flavours will gratify. Today, most people belong to the first category; they find gratification in crudely sexy pin-ups, gaudy kitsch, crass commercial entertainment and raucous music and songs. We cannot call them *rasikas*, as the second kind of viewer, yet in essence this is what they seek to become. Like the *rasika*, they want to taste the flavours of the erotic, the comic, the heroic and so forth. But these are being served up to them in such a way as to further desensitise their palates.

There was a time in India when a large part of the aristocracy and many other citizens were *rasikas*, and when the lower orders enjoyed good art even if they could not explain why. Of course, one of the very big differences between then and now lies in the attitude of the artists. Their sense of responsibility towards their profession and the society they served is clearly suggested by the *Visnudharmottara* when it discusses the responses of different classes of people to art. The list begins with masters of the profession who look for good drawing or articulation of form, the basis of painting and sculpture and the most difficult skill for an artist to acquire. The text continues:

> the connoisseurs praise the display of light and shade, women like the display of ornaments, the rest of the public like richness of colours. Considering this, great care should be taken...so that (a work of art) may be appreciated by everyone.

To sum up the *rasa* theory as a whole, this propounds a system of aesthetic communication dealing with human emotions, values and abstract ideals. It comprehends not only the means by which the artist may communicate them, but also the way they are experienced by the spectator. And it is a system that opens windows onto all historic ages and cultures.

Man is unique not because he does science,
and he is unique not because he does art,
but because science and art equally are expressions of his
marvellous plasticity of mind.

Jacob Bronowski,

As noted earlier, Coomaraswamy interpreted the term *rasa* in two distinct ways: 'ideal beauty' and 'the delight of reason'. Of them the second is perhaps closer to the mark. As the polemicists of old finally agreed, the enrapturing *rasa* experience is intellectual as much as emotional, and Coomaraswamy puts this poetically in a nutshell. But because the *rasa* system is concerned with ideals, and aesthetics with beauty, the former definition stands, even if it is a little abstruse. It also raises a question that needs to be addressed before looking more closely at the individual *rasas*. This concerns the nature of the beautiful and what its laws entail.

The first and most obvious part of the answer is that the concept of beauty changes from age to age and from culture to culture. The concept is determined by several factors, mainly familiarity and necessity. The familiarity factor ought to be clear: if something is new and outlandish, the beholder is so busy trying to fathom it that he is unable to focus properly on its qualities.

The necessity factor can be explained by examples. For the ancient Greeks, muscular athletic bodies were considered ideally beautiful. This was not merely because every four years most able-bodied Greeks participated in the Olympic games; it was more because the Greeks were perpetually at war either among themselves or with neighbouring states, so their young men needed to be fighting fit. In ancient India, by contrast, ideal beauty was seen in the supple, effortless body of the dancer or yogi. To attribute this to a society perpetually at peace would be an exaggeration, but by the Greeks own admission, Indian life was heavenly compared to theirs; while they toiled to produce one crop a year, the Indians produced two or three with a minimum of labour. At least in part this explains why the Indian ideal was mental strength and equilibrium as opposed to physical strength and prowess.

To some extent, too, the concept of beauty changes from individual to individual. While one person sees greater beauty in a red rose, another sees it in a white one, and a third person finds a hibiscus more beautiful than a rose. But the adage 'beauty lies in the eye of the beholder' which is trotted out so frequently has become trite. The man to start it was the Scottish philosopher, David Hume who wrote:

> Beauty is no quality in things themselves: it exists merely in the mind which contemplates them.

But this dictum is more profound than the adage. Inherent in it is a compassion for the things contemplated. A similar compassion and high-mindedness is expressed by Chekhov:

> Everything on earth [is] beautiful, everything, except what we ourselves think and do when we forget the higher purposes of life and our own human dignity.

Yet most people are influenced by the ideals of beauty upheld by their society. And this is even true of the most caring, sensitive and independent minded people. As Stendhal admitted with candour:

> I do not feel I have wisdom enough yet to love what is ugly.

We know that Stendhal was a passionate lover of the beautiful. This reflects in his novels and his writing on art. Yet what he saw as beautiful was established not by him but by his time and culture. If this were not the case he would not have made this remark.

The debate about beauty goes back to the beginning of recorded time. The ancient Egyptians called beauty life, perhaps because survival was almost miraculous in their society. Their contemporaries, the Sumerians, inventors of the earliest script, equated the beautiful and the utilitarian.

There is no known evidence to prove how the people of India's earliest civilisation defined beauty. But if we go by the art objects found at Mohenjodaro, Harappa and analogous sites then we can be sure they agreed with their trading partners, the Sumerians. In fact, Harappan art has a great deal in common with that of the Sumerians, and most of it consists of objects with a practical function.

Most early civilisations upheld the view that the beautiful had to be useful. The Roman rhetorician, Quintilian said:

> The horse that has thin flanks is thought handsomer than one of a different shape, and is also more swift. The athlete whose muscles have been developed by exercise is pleasing to the sight, and is so much the better prepared for the combat. True beauty is never separate from utility.

By Quintilian's time, the Greeks had already added a great deal to the debate. The natural philosophers considered the beautiful and cosmological as one, hence the word 'cosmetic'. The Pythagoreans regarded the universe as a well ordered system; they believed in measuring harmony or beauty by mathematics. For Heraclitus, harmony was dynamic; beauty was found in the unity of conflicting opposites. Such dialectical thinking was common to the Indian materialist philosophers like Charvak; it is also fundamental to early Buddhism.

Plato, too, analysed beauty dialectically: his famous discourse, in which Socrates is the mouthpiece, concludes:

> All that is beautiful is difficult.

111

Plato also equated the beautiful with the good. With respect to art, the most influential Greek was, of course, Aristotle. Defining the laws of beauty, this philosopher said:

> To be beautiful, a living creature, and every whole made of parts, must not only present a certain order in its arrangement of parts, but also be of a certain definite magnitude.

Today, just as ancient Indian aesthetics are disregarded, it is fashionable to dismiss or belittle Aristotle. But for Yuri Borev, the apparently naïve idea that something beautiful is neither too large nor too small is that of a genius and humanitarian because it signifies that beauty is measured in proportion to man.

This is surely a right assessment. When one thinks about it carefully, beautifully proportioned buildings like the Parthenon in Athens, the Great Stupa and Gateways at Sanchi, or the Kailash Temple at Ellora are not so immense as to dwarf people and make them feel insignificant. At the same time they are large enough to remind people of the greatness of their society and its ideals.

In the European Middle Ages, thinkers like Thomas Aquinas and Francis of Assisi believed that beauty had divine origins. In some respects this coincides with the Indian concept of *Satyam Shivam Sundaram*. But in medieval Europe sensual beauty was regarded as sinful, something absolutely alien to Indian philosophy and art.

If one is to make an apt comparison, Indian classical art comes closest to the humanism of the European Renaissance, best exemplified by Leonardo and Shakespeare. Borev points out rightly that in this approach to beauty the artist

> glorified nature and the joy it gives man...

From the mid-18th century, the German philosophers, principally Kant and Hegel, reintroduced dialectical thinking into the concept of the beautiful. For the former, the judgement of beauty is based on feeling and is hence subjective. The latter saw the beautiful as a stage in the evolution of the Universal Spirit. Turning Hegel's idealist system on its head, Marx saw it as a stage in the evolution of material production. In *Economic and Philosophic Manuscripts* he wrote:

> An animal forms objects only in accordance with the standard and need of the species to which it belongs, whilst man knows how to produce in accordance with the standard of every species... Man therefore also forms objects in accordance with the laws of beauty.

The Russian aesthetician, Nikolai Chernyshevsky concluded that beauty is life as it should be. He also postulated the idea that beauty in nature anticipated humanity, a concept that comes close to Indian aesthetics. As already noted, theory demanded that the Indian artist study the forms of nature in order to create the greatest possible beauty and expressiveness in the human figure. So the eyes of a Buddha or Hindu deity are shaped like a bird or the leaves of a particular tree, the fingers like lotus petals, the arms like tapering elephant trunks, and so forth (plate 28).

Though this approach to ideal beauty differs from the Greek, there is in one sense a similarity. The Greek artists did not model an ideal figure on a single person; they put together the best parts of several, in the right order and magnitude, fulfilling Aristotle's dictum. The Indian artists did likewise, putting together the forms drawn from nature into an ordered, well-proportioned whole. And let us not forget that, in the matter of measurement and proportions, the ancient Indians were as precise as the Greeks.

But the final word on beauty should be given to Picasso, the iconoclast supreme of 20th century art who did more than any other artist to banish the Greek ideal from European art. In his typical forthright style he said:

> I hate that aesthetic game of the eye and the mind, played by these connoisseurs, these mandarins who 'appreciate' beauty. What is beauty anyway? There is no such thing.

Yet in the end he surely agrees with David Hume. The compassion for things contemplated may be missing but in its place is colossal indignation at those people of importance - the experts, the 'culturecrats', the collectors, the effete commentators with jaded palates - who presume to appreciate art and endlessly pontificate on it. Such personages abound in the Indian art world and on its peripheries. And the beauty of it all is that many of them seem to have taken Picasso's view all too seriously, finding supreme virtue in ugliness. But as shall soon become clear, there is no such thing as ugliness in art except where work is sloppy and incompetent or where the rules defining art are flouted for the sake of flouting them, or because this is what is prized by the international establishment. And it is ugliness of this sort that is deemed beautiful by the people that count in the art circles of metropolitan India.

There is a fine line dividing opposites, and beauty and ugliness are no exceptions. Perhaps nobody puts it better than Marcel Proust. In his magnum opus, *Remembrance of Things Past*, he says:

> Beauty is a sequence of hypotheses which ugliness cuts short when it bars the way that we could already see opening into the unknown.

114

Apart from what this tells us about the relationship been the two, it also underlines the point made above about beauty and familiarity. Something unfamiliar strikes a discordant note that immediately appears ugly. The element of anticipation is important: beauty warns us that our hypotheses can be false. In other words, beauty is never a conclusive phenomenon.

And what of ugliness? Can this be defined in terms other than as beauty's opposite? Indian aesthetic theory provides some insights. In the *rasa* system the ugly is defined in terms of *bibhatsa*, the odious, a sentiment producing disgust. According to Bharata, this state is determined by hearing, seeing, smelling, tasting, touching or discussing

> unpleasant, offensive, impure and harmful things...

Vishwanatha more graphically mentions

> stinking flesh and fibre and fat...

Interestingly, when the question arises as to how something so vile and ugly could cause aesthetic delight, the Indian theoreticians come close to Aristotle. The latter maintained that while an artwork is always beautiful, it may include ugly images or subjects. About this he said:

> Though the objects themselves may be painful to see, we delight to view the most realistic representation of them in art, the forms for example of the lowest animals and of dead bodies.

The Indian theoreticians, while reiterating this view, were perhaps more conscious of psychology. As B.N. Goswamy notes when discussing the odious *rasa*:

> This transformation of pain into pleasure, possible only through the distance from which the spectator experiences it, is a fact.

> Sights and events painful in themselves do not
> necessarily repel 'when viewed from a psychic
> distance' as the texts say, and are entirely
> capable of yielding an aesthetic experience.

He further notes that in extant examples of the odious *rasa*, mainly miniature paintings, the subject is often the Mother Goddess in her destructive aspect. But because she is a destroyer of evil, the subject is treated with unabashed relish. In the European tradition this finds parallel, for instance, in the work of the Flemish painter, Hieronymus Bosch (c. 1450-1516) whose vast satirical canvases often included the kind of images that would satisfy the Indian definition of the odious and also smack of delight in treatment (plate 23).

Another point to underline is that physical deformity or abnormality is not in principle categorised as odious in the Indian aesthetic system. In fact, in line with the European tradition of freakish clowns and jesters, the Indian tradition categorises dwarves and grotesque pot-bellied fellows as comic. Freakishness can only be categorised as odious if the subject is repugnant, at least in concept.

If the work of any modern artist can make us taste the flavour of *bibhatsa rasa* this is without doubt Francis Bacon. An open homosexual who engaged in sadomasochist acts, Bacon painted canvases that convey an intense feeling of raw, suffering flesh. To enter a room full of his work is to enter a butcher's shop or abattoir. Human figures are trussed like Christmas turkeys, dismembered like lamb or beef, spilling blood and viscera.

Two features redeem Bacon's work from being utterly decadent and unbearable. The first is a corollary of what's already been said about the 'psychic distance' created by art. Of course the point here is that we are talking about art, as opposed to something that pretends to be art. Bacon was not a great master by any means; his draughtsmanship in particular was weak. But this was amply compensated for by the sheer energy of his work and his painterly handling of oil colours.

Bacon's second redeeming feature is protest. In none of his paintings is there a trace of acceptance of the brutality. In some of them the protest rises to a scream, and sometimes it is tinged with pathos or *karuna rasa*. An artwork can embody more than one *rasa* at the same time, although one is always predominant. In Bacon's case the predominant is rarely anything but the odious. In him we find the supreme example of an artist who gave expression to the ugly side of life.

Borev defines the ugly as an aesthetic characteristic with

> a negative significance for society at the present level of its development…

but he feels it is not a serious threat because

> man is able to control the objects possessing this characteristic.

He does, however, remind us that that there exists an extreme degree of the ugly known as the base which is

> embodied in the negative forces which are a menace to humanity, as the people have not yet bent them to their will.

Tyranny is cited as an example of the base. Evil is another word to describe such ugliness.

Clearly Bacon is not base, even if the moralists would have us believe he is. His work contains nothing remotely pornographic. Nor does it glorify evil things, like paedophilia, which seriously menace society.

The kind of 'artworks' we can call base are those that do just that. Not so long ago the Royal Academy of Art in London mounted an exhibition centred on sex, which needless to say attracted mile long queues and earned the Academy a pile. Many of the 'sexhibits' were extremely lurid and the event came under fire from a wide section of the public. What had particularly outraged everybody was the inclusion of portraits of a man and a woman who were evil personified: many years earlier they had been tried and convicted for sexually torturing and murdering children.

Usually it is film that popularises the base in the name of art. Stories of cannibalistic serial killers, violent sexual deviants and mass murderers are all material for smash hits, and if we do not queue up for them at the box office they soon make their way onto the small screen to invade our homes. Their makers and apologists would argue that if we find them distasteful we are not obliged to see them, but this is truly a relinquishment of responsibility. The base exerts a strong fascination for many people. It is only too easy to make capital by pleasing the mob.

This particular form of aesthetic fulfilment is a product of our age. In the past its equivalent was the gladiatorial arena, public executions and other such barbaric entertainments which did away with the niceties of psychic distance.

Since a large percentage of the Indian population has access to satellite television, countless viewers can taste the base almost every day of the week if they so desire. One could also say there are traces of the base in many Bollywood films.

If we think in terms of the horror genre, which at its best can yield a positive, even delightful aesthetic experience, then it appears quite obvious why the odious *rasa* is closely associated with the terrible, to which fear is the key. When talking of fear, Bharata notes that this can arise from

> embarrassment due to offending one's superiors and the king...

Otherwise the determinants of the terrible are listed as:

> Hideous noise, sight of ghosts, panic and anxiety due to... (untimely cry of) jackals and owls, staying in an empty house or forest, sight of death, or captivity of dear ones...

In western theory, one of the most debated of all aesthetic characteristics is the sublime. And because the sublime is something grandiose that inspires fear, it corresponds with, and is an extension of, the terrible sentiment. Germaine Greer sums up the sublime in art when she says:

> A work of sublimity beggars human expectation by being immense beyond human power to realise. Sublimity is often found in natural phenomena, seldom in architecture, sometimes in painting and poetry. Michelangelo's Last Judgement may be described as sublime, simply because it cannot be 'taken in'. The spectator is overpowered, swamped in awe.

The 18th and 19th centuries witnessed a lengthy debate about the relationship between the sublime and the beautiful. The Irish-born philosopher and statesman, Edmund Burke defined the two as distinct phenomena; he identified beauty with the delicate and harmonious and the sublime with the vast, obscure, and terrifying. Because of the fear factor, Kant saw the sublime as a kind of negative beauty. And Hegel saw it as yet another stage in the evolution of the Universal Spirit, represented by the Romantic Movement in art.

Wild and mysterious nature, faraway exotic lands and melodramatic subjects like shipwrecks and battles constituted the sublime in the art of the Romantics. But today the horizons of the sublime have expanded literally to infinity. Awe is now inspired by nuclear power, the exploration of space and our expanding knowledge of the origins of the universe. As Borev puts it:

> The infinity and eternity of the world, the enormous inner power of nature and man, unlimited prospects for the exploration of nature and its humanisation - all this is a manifestation of the sublime as a category of aesthetics.

Borev also asserts that the sublime is a phenomenon

> affecting the life of nations or mankind as a whole.

And he divides it into the positive, which enhances the power of man, and the negative, which reduces it.

The first moon landing or the discovery of DNA can be cited as examples of the positive side of the sublime. An example of the negative side is nuclear destruction. In the words of Donald Hornig, a witness to the first atomic test:

> Aside from being tremendous it was one of the most aesthetically beautiful things I have ever seen.

In art, Borev finds examples of the sublime in the music of Beethoven:

> Grandiose and infinite... sudden, unexpected... tempestuous explosions, the whispers of love and the roar of global cataclysms. The epoch of revolutionary upheavals has stormed its way into music and changed it.

He also sees the sublime in Gothic cathedrals which

> soaring upwards... personified the link
> between man's hopes and god.

Seen in this light, Greer's observation that the sublime is rare in architecture is inaccurate. Certainly it does not hold in India where so many sacred monuments fill one with awe. The excavated cave sanctuaries at both Ajanta and Elephanta are supreme examples.

At Ajanta, an initial tasting of the sublime is experienced as one first contemplates from afar the whole complex of prayer halls and monasteries, carved into the interior of a horseshoe shaped hill. The feeling of awe is heightened if one is present there in the monsoon season when the landscape is clothed in a mantle of myriad greens of psychedelic intensity. Waterfalls cascade down the rock face between the caves; in the gorge below the river roars like a tiger after which it was named; above and opposite, bountiful clouds kiss the ridge of the hills. The moment of taking all this in is overwhelming.

The immediate surrounds of the temples on the island of Elephanta are not quite so dramatic, but it is with a sense of apprehension that one enters their interiors. As one's vision adjusts to the darkness, grandiose and mysterious sculpted images slowly reveal themselves; in taking full cognisance of the towering Shiva *Trimurti* one is again overawed. At Ajanta, the first sight of the painted murals and the massive presence of the Buddha produce a similar experience. It is only when one contemplates each work individually that one tastes other flavours of *rasa*.

There are many who may say that the Taj Mahal offers an experience of the sublime. But for true connoisseurs of Mughal architecture, this experience may be found in two other structures or complex of structures : Humayun's Tomb in New Delhi and the city built by Akbar at Fathepur Sikri. While the former inspires awe with its massiveness and the stark simplicity of its lines, the latter makes its impact with its grandiose, unified design and with its position atop a hill that looks onto endless plains and farmlands fanning out in every direction.

The finest of Indian musicians like the late Amir Khan, Ali Akbar Khan, Ravi Shankar or Kishori Amonkar also at times express the sublime. Of course, Indian classical music corresponds to the *rasa* system, with every *raga* creating a mood appropriate to the time of day, the season and so forth. But sometimes, the Indian musicians creates a sound that seems to emanate from the depths of the earth, sombre and grave, and then rises with slow certainty towards the heavens.

In the films of Ritwik Ghatak there are many moments of the sublime. In *Meghe Dhake Tara* (The Cloud-Capped Star), when the dying heroine cries out her desire to live, the hills reverberate with her anguished sound. In *Komal Gandhar*, as a train crashes to a halt at a barrier marking the divide between the two Bengals, one hears the refrain of women's voices, like the chorus in a Greek tragedy, lamenting the cutting in two of the earth. Later, at the end of the same film, the hero and heroine join hands on the bank of a river, symbolic of the reunification of Bengal that Ghatak believed both necessary and inevitable. All these sequences are of such majesty as to induce goose flesh in the sensitive spectator.

Picasso's *Guernica* (plate 4) has been discussed in another context, but if one analyses the painting according to *rasa*, then one may immediately perceive that its predominant sentiment is the terrible. At the same time, the work communicates a feeling of profound sorrow and grief, expressions of *karuna rasa*, the pathetic sentiment.

If there is anything common underlying the expression of the terrible or sublime throughout the ages this is loneliness and vulnerability. Bharata talks of fear of the powerful, fear of ghosts, isolation, death and captivity. The Romantic artists such as Goya, Géricault and Delacroix painted human beings, imprisoned, awaiting death, confronting the savagery of nature and war. Turner painted landscape as it had never been painted before: almost abstract like the quantum physicists equations, full of foreboding, vast and unfathomable, as if to predict the discoveries of the 20th century.

In some respects, the *rasa* of the marvellous, *adbhuta*, comes close to the sublime. Corresponding to the emotional state of astonishment or wonder, this *rasa* is determined, according to the ancient texts, by the sight of unearthly beings and entry into grandiose monuments like a temple, audience hall or palace. Bharata adds the following determinants to the list:

> magic, extraordinary feats of men, great excellence in painting, art, works in parchment and the like.

This list is very significant on two counts. Firstly it acknowledges that the experience of great art is classified on a par with witnessing heroic actions and rare human accomplishments. Therefore, in it we find confirmation of the lofty place accorded to art in that age.

Secondly, it indicates that art was seen in the same light as magic, a view quite in line with modern thinking on the subject. Ernst Fischer's statement on the subject, elsewhere quoted, may be recalled. In this context, too, one can cite the Kailash Temple at Ellora, the largest monolithic structure in the world. This produces a feeling best summed up by its unknown architect. According to an inscription, he was so struck with wonder by his own creation that his heart failed him when he considered building another, and so he asked himself:

> How is it possible that I built this except by magic?

From our modern perspective, by far the most significant point implied by Bharata is that all art of excellence - no matter what the flavour - makes the sensitive spectator or *rasika* experience the flavour of the marvellous. This accords exactly with the modern interpretation of art and magic. When, through sleight of hand, the conjuror creates a moment of illusion, the spectator wonders how he did it. And so it is with art. When an artwork successfully communicates ideas and feelings the spectator is struck with wonder and asks herself or himself how the artist achieved it. And the more skilful and original the artist is, the more the spectator marvels.

But if, on the other hand, a painting, play or poem, a film or piece of music give no room for wonder, then can they justly be called works of art? One of the main functions of art is to reveal, to help people see, hear and understand things they have not perceived in quite the same way before. Even a small, apparently insignificant work can be a revelation.

In view of Bharata's evidently advanced understanding of this fundamental aspect of art perception, it is somewhat surprising that little importance was given to the marvellous sentiment by most subsequent theoreticians. One of the exceptions was Narayana, the great-grandfather of Vishwanatha. Narayana viewed *adbhuta* as the only *rasa* because, according to his analysis, everything else proceeds from it and merges into it. This corresponds closely to the modern understanding of the magical experience of art.

Among ancient Indian artworks, one that best characterises the marvellous *rasa* is a sculpture from Mathura (plate 14).

A work of considerable theatricality, it almost certainly represents an episode in the story of the first sexual experience of the boy ascetic, Rishyashringa. In both Buddhist and Hindu literature the adolescent sage lives in a hermitage and is unaware of the existence of the opposite sex; taking advantage of his innocence, a celestial nymph seduces him (plate 21). The work in question portrays the boy after his seduction, a miraculous experience that has filled him with wonder and delight. One cannot speak for the experience of the *rasika* of yore, but the wonder and delight the work creates today is due to the depth of feeling it communicates; while the figure of the young sage is worldly and non-ascetic, his expression of wonder is full of innocence and tenderness.

Memorial to Builders by Anil Karanjai (see title page, Art & Politics) provides a modern example of the marvellous. The painting makes an indirect political statement by highlighting the forgotten people who built India's great historic monuments, which are always attributed to mighty rulers. Although the figures entrapped in stone speak of suffering and sacrifice, they standout in relief to accuse their oppressors. It is through their ghostly presence that *adbhuta* arises, giving the spectator cause for wonder.

In the canon of *rasa*, the heroic and the furious flavours have much in common, a commonness that makes sense when one thinks of contemporary action films like *Rambo* or an Amitabh Bachchan blockbuster. A wronged man, burning with rage, takes revenge by taking up arms against the perpetrators of evil and generally cleansing society; he thereby becomes an ideal or model for lesser mortals, incapable of translating their anger into heroic action.

In Greek mythology heroes - and, indeed, heroines - were demi-divinities who find parallels in Indian mythology. They were believed to have lived on earth in distant dim ages when they went through adventures and ordeals, performing great services for human civilisation, as did Lords Ram and Krishna. The destruction of monsters, the liberation of the oppressed, the establishment of peace and order were their main tasks. And as with the Indian gods and demi-gods, the legends of their deeds provided a wealth of material to artists and poet-dramatists.

Of course, the superhuman feats of the heroes demanded many qualities other than mere physical strength and anger. The list, in fact, is exhaustive. But if we turn back to Indian aesthetics, Bharata et al, we find reference to many of them. Among the qualities associated with the hero, Bharata lists:

> absence of sadness, power, patience, determination... steadiness, munificence, boldness, firmness... charity, diplomacy...

Defining the difference between the furious and the heroic, Bharata says that while the former arises from anger which belongs to everybody, the latter arises from energy and belongs to superior people. This is a definition that corresponds to Aristotle's thoughts on anger:

> It is easy to fly into a passion, anybody can do that but to be angry with the right person and to the right extent and at the right time and with the right object and in the right way that is not easy, and it is not everyone who can do it.

On the subject of the furious *rasa*, Bharata further notes that its determinants include:

rape, abuse, insult, untrue allegations...
threatening, revengefulness, jealousy...

He also classifies anger into five categories, each differently expressed:

anger caused by enemies, superior persons, lovers, servants and feigned anger.

How closely all this corresponds to our modern reality.

But on quite another note, Bharata also talks of demons, the *rakshasas* and *danavas*, whose fury he defines as intrinsic to their existence. His description of these demons is highly theatrical:

They are naturally furious, for they have many arms, many mouths, standing and unkempt hairs of brown colour, and prodigious physical frames of black complexion...

The comic vision this description conjures up is not out of place because in the theatre such characters can only be played by fine comedians.

In Indian painting and sculpture, the furious is most frequently represented by images of deities slaying an adversary, for example, the Goddess Durga, Shiva in his destructive aspect and Vishnu's man-lion incarnation, Narasimha. But most of these images are also characterised by energy which brings them into the realm of the heroic. This is why the distinction between the furious and heroic *rasas* is considered so subtle.

When discussing the differences between the two in visual representations Goswmay observes that, in contrast to anger,

energy is directed not necessarily against a given adversary...but informs the very person of a hero... Among the most moving renderings of energy are those assertive,

> monumental portraits...which
> emphasize...the might, the dignity, the air of
> authority that belong to a noble personage.

An example of this kind of portrait is a male head, probably a warrior, belonging to the Kushana era (plate 7).

Among works belonging to the European tradition probably nothing better exemplifies both the heroic and the furious than Michelangelo's monumental sculpture of the biblical King David. The giant killer's face (plate 8) speaks so eloquently of these two flavours that further words are unnecessary. The only thing to add is that such an example underscores the point that the *rasa* system is applicable to every culture at any point in history.

The timelessness and universality of the *rasa* system does not imply that everything one can say about it applies to all art everywhere. It is axiomatic that between cultures and historic ages there are numerous variations in forms of aesthetic expression, and these are sometimes subtle, sometimes vast. What remain unchanging are essential human values or ideals and basic human feelings. The way of expressing these is the variant.

Between the Indian and European traditions one large area of difference lies in the approach to tragedy. It is only natural that this should be so, for of all forms of aesthetic expression, tragedy is the most complex and the most closely tied to the overall philosophical outlook of a people. As Yuri Borev puts it:

> Tragedy is a philosophical art which poses
> and solves metaphysical problems of life, tries
> to grasp its meaning and analyses global
> problems...

Borev then goes on to offer an explanation of the opposing eastern and western approaches to tragedy. According to his analysis, two extreme positions have been evolved by world art when treating tragic situations: existential and Buddhist. He says that the existentialist

> regards death as the central problem of philosophy and art... life and death... (as) equally absurd.

In outlining the second position Borev makes reference to reincarnation:

> Buddhism maintains that after death man becomes another being... therefore his death does not really change anything.

One wonders why he mentions only Buddhism in this context. Perhaps a rudimentary knowledge of Sanskrit drama led him to believe that other Indian philosophies are unconcerned with tragedy. This apart, there are strands of Buddhist thought strongly suggesting that belief in reincarnation was not central to the Buddha's original philosophy. All that one can say with certainty is that suffering was its starting point. Without a rude awakening to the tragedy of disease, ageing and death, we would have had no Buddha. And whatever the shortcomings in Borev's logic, it can be said that the Indian philosophical outlook has traditionally equipped people to cope better with tragedy.

But does this explain why in Indian tradition there are no tragedies in the Greek or existential sense, no works of art in which the entire focus is death? To some extent, perhaps. The need for catharsis may be less acute when people view death as a mere act in the drama of life rather than as something finite and fearful.

For a more complete answer to this question one must first better understand the dynamics of tragedy in the western

129

aesthetic tradition. And the first thing to note is that this is essentially heroic. It was Scott Fitzgerald who said:

> Show me a hero, and I will write you a tragedy.

And his words are echoed by Arthur Miller:

> The tragic feeling is evoked in us when we are in the presence of a character who is ready to lay down his life, if need be, to secure one thing his sense of personal dignity.

In ancient Greece, the themes from which the tragedian drew were almost without exception the heroic or epic myths and legends. This meant that the plots were very well known to the public. So what made tragedy so compelling and so popular? Bertolt Brecht provides part of the answer in *A Short Organum For The Theatre*. Speaking in the context of Greek tragedy he says:

> Theatre may be said to be derived from ritual, but...it becomes theatre once the two have separated; what it brought over from the mysteries was not its former ritual function, but purely and simply the pleasure which accompanied this.

As with all theatre, all art, the pleasure of Greek tragedy derived from two inseparable sources: form and content. Great poetic language, much of it delivered by a chorus, a rich cast of characters including oracles, and a narrative suited to the amphitheatre were among the main components of the first. As to content, audiences were thrilled, not by the story, but by the way it unfolded. As Borev puts it:

> The message of the whole lay in not the unavoidable and fateful denouement but in the hero's actions. The motive forces of the plot and the results of the hero's actions were laid bare... It was not fate which carried the

hero to the finale; his tragic destiny was his own doing.

The audience's empathy with the hero and his fatal flaw constituted the thrill, giving rise to catharsis.

In the European Middle Ages, the tenor of tragedy shifted to martyrdom, reflecting the suffering of Christ and his persecuted followers. In the paintings and stories of martyrs or ill-fated lovers such as Tristram and Iseult, suffering and death were not the responsibility of the doomed; they were brought on by the will of god. The purpose here was not catharsis but consolation; spectators could console themselves that god had treated them more kindly than the doomed even though they were less deserving.

The emphasis on the supernatural and miraculous in medieval tragedies was replaced by the realism of the Renaissance. While Christ's suffering was made human in painting and sculpture, tragedies like Hamlet, Othello and Romeo and Juliet were the stories of individuals unrestricted by fate or faith. Highlighting the differences between these and earlier tragedies Borev states:

> Renaissance man sought to explain (the world) and its tragedies through the world itself... The world, including the domain of human relations, passions and tragedies, does not require a supernatural explanation;... to explain everything by the intrinsic qualities of things, to derive everything from its own material nature, that was the spirit of the new realism which found the most complete expression in Shakespeare's tragedies.

The hope held out by Renaissance humanism for a harmonious personality - the creatively and emotionally liberated individual - was not long lived. It was nipped in the bud by what Borev describes as

> the icy wind of bourgeois individualism...

131

Borev believes that great writers like Rabelais, Cervantes and Shakespeare had a premonition of this tragedy. And in this he may be right. But what none of them could have foreseen was the extent or duration of the tragedy. They could not have guessed that over the coming five centuries and more, the bourgeois winds would blow - icy, lukewarm, hot or cold - in every corner of the world, rendering it and individuals ever more fragmented, ever less harmonious.

It is altogether another world one must enter when talking of tragedy and Indian tradition. Whatever the many shortcomings of ancient Indian society, this was integrated to an extent unimaginable today. Even a divisive system like caste was evidently not applied with any degree of intensity. And even economic divisions were not so wide as to threaten social harmony. Food was generally abundant, as was land; and cultivators could not be evicted from the land they tilled, a right removed by the British, with whom blew the bourgeois winds.

Many contemporary historians and other intellectuals are cynical about such a picture of India's past, as if anyone who paints it is a *Hindutva* ideologue, a champion of Hindu nationalism. To counter this, if one brings up the subject of art and aesthetics, pointing out that these reflect more harmonious times, the argument tends to be forwarded that classical Indian art was idealistic and did not reflect reality. This, as much as the *Hindutva* view, is not only so ignorant as to be laughable but also an insult to the intelligence of the artists and scientists of the past.

Ideals, like myths, whether Indian, Greek or Hottentot are rooted in reality and if one society emphasises a particular ideal or aesthetic genre more than another there are good reasons for it. Why the ancient Indians did not create tragic heroes like Oedipus and Agamemnon, is perhaps beyond the scope of the present discussion. It would be tempting to conclude that this land was fortunate enough not to have kings who mistakenly married their mothers or intentionally sacrificed their daughters for victory in war. But one cannot be certain that this was the case. What one can assert is that the ancient Indians did not create tragic heroes, not because they were effete fellows lost in the concept of illusion or *maya*, but because their culture and society had no demand for such heroes, no need for catharsis.

Most interestingly, however, Aristotle's much quoted theory on tragedy comes strikingly close to one aspect of the *rasa* system. He said that the purpose of tragedy is to act as

> a purgative of the emotions by means of pity
> and terror.

Pity and terror: *karuna,* the *rasa* of pathos and compassion, and *bhayanaka*, the *rasa* of the terrible. Of course, the experience of catharsis is the very antithesis of the tasting of *rasa*; while the one is a cleansing out, the other is a relishing, a taking in, and this reflects a much more sensuous culture. Yet, in the final analysis, they both give pleasure.

A few words are now due on the specifics of *karuna*, because this is the *rasa* corresponding to the tragic. The mood or emotion arising from this flavour is sorrow and its determinants according to Bharata include:

> affliction under a curse, separation from dear
> ones, loss of wealth, death, captivity, flight,
> accidents or any other misfortune.

Obviously, since there are no tragedies in Indian art, such situations only occur as part of a narrative that ends happily. Sanskrit drama includes numerous sad and melodramatic scenes designed to evoke *karuna* rasa, but the philosophy behind these was that sad or tragic events belong to the cycle of life.

The visual arts followed the same conventions, and this is most apparent in the art of the Buddhist monuments. The *Jataka* tales and stories from the Buddha's life, which in their time were also performed, constitute the narrative at Buddhist sites. The theme underlying many of them is tragic, giving rise to *karuna rasa* (plate 11). But in all the stories protection and solace are found in the Compassionate One, either a *Bodhisattva* or the Buddha himself.

In the ancient texts, there are elaborate discussions on the relationship between *karuna rasa* and the state of sorrow evoked by love. As many as ten different conditions exist for lovers separated from their beloved and these are treated as pathetic by writers. But many agree that sorrow arising from love in separation differs from that leading to *karuna rasa* because, however deep it might be, it does not imply finality. As Bharata explains:

> The pathetic sentiment relates to a condition
> of despair, while the erotic sentiment based on
> separation relates to a condition of retaining
> optimism arising out of yearning and anxiety.

The depiction of lovers in separation was a much favoured theme in miniature paintings.

In the light of what was earlier remarked on Renaissance tragedies, it is important to note that tragic romances became popular in Indian art from the 17th century, for example, *Laila and Majnun* and *Sassi and Punnu*. As importantly, these come close to Renaissance humanism, for inherent in them is a good deal of critical realism. This is an area which requires further exploration, but it may in the meantime give a little more weight to the suggestion elsewhere discussed that capitalism was evolving in India under Mughal rule.

In the post Renaissance era, much of the art created in Europe reflected the tragedy of the ever more fragmented world and individual. Though tragedy had disappeared as a genre by the 19th century, tragic elements continued to underlie the work of many major artists. The Romantics, for instance, expressed themselves through sublimity or terror, but at the base of the terror was the tragedy brought on by the expanding industrial revolution, urbanisation and the uprooting of countless individuals. From this time on, tragedy became more and more of a collective phenomenon. The example of the pianist and composer, Frederic Chopin is apt. The profound sadness of his music was not only personal, but also an expression of nostalgia and grief for Poland, where he had roots, a land suffering tragic political events.

Although it may appear paradoxical, tragedy is analysed as positive, even optimistic by many western philosophers. In his treatise on the subject, David Hume pointed out that the tragic emotion has elements of

> grief, joy, horror and pleasure

And while Hegel attributed everything to the hero's tragic flaw, Marx placed heroic sacrifice in the context of a revolutionary conflict, which changes society.

Expanding upon Hume, Borev says that tragic art

> is a mournful song about an irreplaceable loss and a joyous hymn to the immortality of man... (it) reveals the social meaning of man's life showing that his immortality is realised through the immortality of his people.

He also emphasises that the typical structure of a work of tragic art is

> suffering-death-grief-joy

In the ultimate analysis, this is not so very far from the cyclical character of Indian art.

One final point on tragedy made by Borev relates to the characteristic known as the horrible. About this the lucid aesthetician says:

> Tragedy is optimistic, while the horrible is hopeless and endless... nothing to make it bearable, nothing to show that the horror will be over... In the tragic, the affliction is sublime, it ennobles man who remains the master of the situation and asserts his rule over the world even in death. In the horrible, man is the slave of circumstances.

The world outlook and art of the medieval period are fitting examples of the horrible, as are the writings of Franz Kafka. While in the first the enslavement is by God and the Church, in Kafka humanity is the victim of regimes or systems controlled by faceless men.

In Indian art, as already noted, tragedy as a genre first appeared in the pre-colonial era. That this did not evolve during the subsequent centuries is quite clearly not a reflection of India's reality under British rule. But it does reflect the overall cultural decline resulting from that reality.

With the emergence of a national consciousness, particularly in Bengal, expressions of the tragic came to the fore. The Bengal famine, a man-made event, was taken up by artists like Chittaprasad (plate 12) and Gobardhan Ash and again, after independence, by Satyajit Ray. Tragedy also underlay many Bombay films of the same era. Bimal Roy and Guru Dutt are but two of the directors who made powerful films on tragic themes.

Yet without any shadow of doubt the great Indian tragedians of this age are Sadat Hasan Manto and Ritwik Ghatak. And what inspired their art was one of the greatest of all modern political tragedies: the Partition of India in 1947. Manto's Partition stories are mainly focused on the communal violence in the Punjab and Bombay, and he relates them with a brutal irony worthy of Balzac. But at times he also betrays a compassion for his characters and in this, as in his versatility, he is often reminiscent of Guy de Maupassant, one of the greatest short story writers of all times.

In Ghatak's films, the focus is on middle-class refugee families in post-Partition Bengal. The ruthlessly critical way he unveils his characters, unable to cope with their new impoverishment and proletarian status, is matched with a deep sympathy for his heroines whose fate he seems to equate with the tragedy of divided Bengal.

In Ghatak's final, autobiographical film, the protagonist is killed in police-rebel crossfire during the Naxalite uprising. Ghatak's own fatal flaw - his love for the bottle - underlies the tragedy. But he makes it clear in the end that it is his inability to compromise that has fuelled the flaw. Therefore, his sacrifice is ultimately revolutionary. A character like Ghatak was probably the farthest thing from Marx's mind when he conceived his tragic hero. But revolutions are like the world: it takes all sorts to make them.

One can seriously assert that of all the aesthetic flavours embraced by the *rasa* system, the one which links cultures and levels people more than any other is the comic. Love stories or romances are also universal but they can be tragic or comic depending on the outcome; they can also be dramatic or melodramatic, which entails the tasting of almost every flavour. And tragedy, as we have seen, is culture specific and has tended to set heroes apart from the rest.

The universal and unifying nature and role of the comic does not of course mean that it has neither cultural and historic characteristics nor different shades and nuances. But what it does mean in Borev's words is that:

> the essence of the comic is always the same...
> The comic condemns the imperfections of life,
> purifies and renovates man and asserts the
> joys of living.

The creative aspect of laughter was evidently so well understood by the ancient Egyptians that, according to a papyrus, they attributed the creation of the world to the laughter of the gods. For the Greeks, with their understanding of the need for catharsis, it was almost obligatory for people to let their hair down at least once a year in an orgy of drinking, ribaldry and laughter. They believed that Dionysus, their god of wine and vegetation, was benign to those who followed him, but brought madness and destruction upon those who spurned his cult. The Romans had the equivalent of Dionysian festivals in their Saturnalia, a periodic return to the Golden Age of impropriety when anything could be ridiculed and slaves were served by their masters. India's spring festival, Holi is also a Saturnalia although it has tended to become corrupted in modern times.

To say that tragedy and comedy are two sides of the same mask is to repeat what is very well known. But a few words on a lesser known aspect of their oneness would be useful here. One of the principles underlying tragedy, and one of the reasons tragedy is in the ultimate optimistic, is resurrection. From our modern standpoint this is interpreted as a hero living on in the people after his death. But for the ancients whose economy depended on agriculture it was the gods like Dionysus who died and rose from the dead, like a seed that is buried in order to become a life-giving plant. Comedy, too, is based on the principle, not exactly of resurrection, but of renovation or renewal; this

138

time, however, the renewal is not of a deity or hero, but of the human being.

Seen in this light, the rationale of the most important Dionysian festival becomes clear. Held in Athens for five days each spring, the celebrations encompassed not only ritual orgies packed with fun and laughter but also dramatic performances and competitions; the genre of the dramas was not comedy but tragedy. Indeed, the great tragedians, Aeschylus, Sophocles and Euripides wrote their plays for this festival.

Aristotle noted that comedy in Greece developed considerably later than tragedy. He also noted that in ancient Athens it was regarded as an inferior dramatic form. This was no doubt on account of the aristocratic appeal of tragedy and the popular appeal of comedy. Yet there are records to show that burlesque and parody coexisted with tragedy and that the subject ridiculed could be drawn from tragedies performed at the competitions. These must have been hugely popular with the general public, the lower orders, who have always loved to see fun poked at the ruling elite. Probably the elite too enjoyed this form of entertainment and had the self-confidence to laugh at their own foibles.

In the Indian aesthetic system, there is no precise equivalent of the Greek comedy. Instead there is *hasya rasa*, the comic flavour or sentiment. But in many respects this bears a similarity to the parody that evolved in Greece. In *Laughing Matters*, a brilliant study of the comic tradition in India, Lee Siegel explains:

> The comic sentiment...arises out of an opposition to, or parody of, any of the other aesthetic flavours. It is... experienced when something tastes funny, when representations of the emotions of love or courage or sadness fail to produce the corresponding and expected amorous, heroic or tragic *rasas*. The

comic *Ganas* are born out of the ashes of the sublime. They mock heroes and lovers, sages and saints...

Siegel also notes that the comic parodies not only the other *rasas* but also itself. An example of this would be a take-off of a bad comedian or someone relating an unfunny joke.

Apart from the passion and wit with which it is written, what makes *Laughing Matters* compelling and compulsory reading is the wealth of material discussed by the author; this reveals ancient Indian comedy to have been as bawdy and irreverent as any comedy anywhere and at any time could be. Siegel explains why most of the world has been deprived of its pleasures:

> The puritanical scholarship of the pioneers of Indian studies created an impression that, while there was ample truth and beauty, elegance and wisdom, in Sanskrit literature, there was little humor or satire. The standard surveys of Sanskrit literature... lacking any appreciation of vulgarity, perpetuated the assumption that the vast literature was devoid of a comic sensibility... (They) inevitably contained stern and sober judgements of those ribald texts.

Given the reluctance of most Indians to mock the powerful or established institutions, this is hardly surprising. No-one or nothing is sacred in the comic tradition, including the gods and religion itself. To give a mild example, in Sudraka's *Mrcchakatika* (*The Little Clay Cart*), written around the 4th century, the *vidusaka* or jester asks:

> What's the use of worshipping the gods? They don't bother to show any favour no matter how much you worship them...

Consider, too, the words of Bharata on the subject of his sons:

> Once they had mastered the Scripture of Dramatic Arts, my sons began to ridicule everyone in the entire universe with farces... and soon they performed a satire of the Divine Sages, a play full of vulgarities.

The comic *Ganas*, Shiva's pot-bellied troops, are paragons of vulgarity and they set out to mock all forms of decency and refinement. As Siegel comments when discussing the *Ganas*:

> Comedy is an affront to delicacy. It is a deliverance from the tyranny of beauty. The comic *rasa* demands a savoring of bad taste.

Sex of different varieties, genitalia, farting and other scatological references are all brought into play with sparkling naughtiness. Some of it is so risqué and irreverent to the gods that if it were performed or written today the concerned parties would be pursued hell for leather all at once by the VHP, the RSS and the Bajrang Dal and sundry others of their mindset, probably including most of the current Cabinet.

However, it must be said that the kind of low buffoonery in question belongs to a time. A very similar form of satire is the basis of the oeuvre of the great Greek, Aristophanes, but to write such plays today would be inappropriate. The art of the past belongs to a time and a social context. We can appreciate it today but we cannot repeat it. Both the plays of the Greek and the comic flavour in Sanskrit drama belong to an age of relative innocence to which we can never return. Nor can we quote them out of context.

To make this point clearer, let us focus for a moment on the controversy that arose a few years ago over the Hindi song, *Choli ke piche kya hai?* (What's underneath her blouse?) from the film, *Khalnayak* directed by Subhash Ghai. This was adapted from a Rajasthani folk song, and many people defended it on the grounds that the original was never deemed vulgar even though Rajasthani village society is as conservative as any society can be. What nobody pointed out is that in a traditional rural society, still uncorrupted by brutal urban norms, sexual suggestiveness is not offensive or threatening, while in a brutalised urban society, robbed of every vestige of innocence, it leads to acts harmful to women and, by extension, to society in general.

Returning to the comic, what remains constant to this flavour, no matter what its cultural references, is its democratic, radical character. As George Orwell wrote:

> A thing is funny when in some way that is not actually offensive or frightening it upsets the established order. Every joke is a tiny revolution... whatever destroys dignity and brings down the mighty from their seats, preferably with a bump, is funny.

There are many different shades of the comic: jokes and puns; banter and raillery; wit and repartee; irony and sarcasm; farce and burlesque; caricature and cartoon; satire and humour; parody and impersonation... The list seems almost endless, and the differences between the shades are sometimes blatant and sometimes subtle. But, implicitly or explicitly, all of them are critical of things as they are.

Historically no other form of aesthetic expression has offered artists more critical scope. The comic has allowed them to take an anti-establishment stand, often an extreme one, with far greater effect and, on the whole, with much less risk than direct criticism. Borev outlines a probable reason:

> The essence of the comic is contradiction... (It) is criticism which both rejects and asserts. Laughter seeks to do away with a world full of injustice and replace it with a better one. It implies both destruction and creative construction.

The comic as a weapon against the ills of society has taken a wide variety of forms at different historical moments. In the European context, mention has already been made of the mandatory laughter and parodies of the Dionysian festival and the Roman Saturnalia, as well as the risqué satire of Aristophanes. Another ancient form of the comic was the brainchild of Aesop, who related teasing fables to incite slaves to rebellion. Much later, under the oppressive feudalism of the Middle Ages, carnivals became the people's outlet. This culture is colourfully summed up by Borev:

> ...laughter opposing the rigid ideas spread by
> the official church sounded during carnivals,
> at comical pageants and processions, festivals
> of fools and asses, in parodies, in the frivolous
> language of the street, in the witticisms and
> pranks of jesters...

Among medieval poets, the comic reached its heights in Geoffrey Chaucer, just as tragedy had risen supreme in Dante.

The violence and upheavals of the Renaissance inspired many painters to express themselves in the satiric mode. One finds examples in the grotesque canvases of Bosch and the critical realism of the German, Lucas Cranach. In Shakespeare, the contradictions of comedy found new expression in the clowns and fools of his tragedies.

One of the greatest all time satirists was undoubtedly Molière. Frequently in trouble with the powers that be - the Catholic Church and the absolutist regime of his patron, Louis XIV - Molière's comedies hit at the heart of ruling class hypocrisy and the mores and manners of the rising bourgeoisie. Two centuries later, another Frenchman, Honoré Daumier became the father of the modern cartoon (plate 1). Yet another artist to find expression in the comic was Francisco Goya, a master of the satirical grotesque (plate 3). Three modern masters of this genre were the German Expressionists, George Grosz (plate 5), Max Ernst and Max Beckmann.

Among satirical playwrights, the most important figure of the 20th century was Brecht who, like the Expressionists, grew to artistic maturity under the evil shadow of Nazism. As noted in relation to Greek tragedy, Brecht insisted that even the most serious of subjects should be pleasurable:

> From the first it has been the theatre's business to entertain people, as it also has of all the other arts. It is this business which always gives it its particular dignity; it needs no other passport than fun...

Brecht's philosophy echoes in Charlie Chaplin, the most towering of all 20th century comedians. Indeed, Chaplin is much more than that, for in him the figure of the tragic clown finds the most perfect form of universal expression. He is also the closest we will ever get to the complete work of art, meaning that his work encompasses all the arts: the silent images of painting; the narrative of literature; music, theatre and dance; and finally film, the art form of our times.

In Chaplin, too, we find both humour and satire, which, as Borev underlines, are two distinct comic forms:

> The object of humour is not above criticism but is on the whole quite attractive. Everything rotten is the object of satire.

Lee Siegel expresses the same understanding in a very different way:

> Satire is laughter at the vices and follies to which humanity is driven by the agonies of old age, disease, and death; humor is laughter in spite of disease, in acceptance of old age, in surrender to death.

Those familiar with Buddhism may recognise here a response to a question attributed to Gautama:

> How can anyone laugh who knows of old age, disease and death?

Brecht echoes the future Buddha in one of his poems:

> The man who laughs
> Has simply not yet [heard]
> The terrible news.

Perhaps nobody answers Gautam's question better than the American comedian, Lenny Bruce. Bruce's epigraph reads:

> People should be taught what is, not what should be. All my humor is based on destruction and despair. If the whole world were tranquil, without disease and violence, I'd be standing in the bread line right back of J. Edgar Hoover.

As an optimistic philosopher, Borev puts it quite differently:

> Comedy is the fruit of advanced civilisation...
> A sense of humour is a feature of an aesthetically developed mind.

With this observation in mind it is fascinating to note that aesthetically developed minds were at work in India perhaps as much as 10,000 years ago. In the central state of Madhya Pradesh, which is rich in Stone Age sites, there are paintings clearly marked by elements of the comic. One such example is the image titled *Dancing Wizards* (plate 9), already discussed for its mathematically harmonious composition. The whole work evidently represents a ritual dance-drama. The willowy figure to the left with feathered head-dress is a harbinger of Shiva Nataraja, the Lord of Dance. To the right, a youthful figure leaps into space with the vim and easy grace of a master ballet dancer. In the foreground, the standing figure with a bison-horned mask, curves his head and torso towards the seated figure with a wolf's mask and claw; the two are playfully taunting one another in the style of European medieval mummers (plate 10). It is wonderful to think that the comic flavour could be expressed with such delight in the Mesolithic Age, when an advanced civilisation was still millennia in the future.

As noted, Bharata's *Natyashastra* was written around the 2nd century AD. But in common with so many other ancient Indian texts, its contents were compiled from a long tradition. The comic being a popular form, rooted in folk theatre and art, must have had a particularly long history. In any case, together with *shringara*, the erotic or amorous flavour, the comic *rasa* is given a place of the greatest importance by Bharata. Discussing *hasya rasa* in all its nuances, he categorises six different kinds of laughter and three different kinds of laughers:

> To persons of the superior type belong the slight smile and the smile; to those of the middling type, the gentle laughter and the laughter of ridicule, and to those of the inferior type the vulgar...excessive laughter.

One cannot know whether this was written with an element of tongue in cheek, but it does tell us something about the responses of different social classes to the comic. Given the kind of naughtiness and irreverence discussed above, one may well imagine that in the main it was the lower classes that laughed holding their bellies and baring their teeth when tasting the flavour of the comic. As Oliver Goldsmith noted:

> We only laugh at those instances of moral absurdity to which we are conscious we ourselves are not liable.

While the *rasa* theory makes clear distinctions between the tasting of aesthetic flavours and the feelings experienced in life, exception is made for the comic. According to the theoreticians, people laugh at the same things and in the same way both in art and life. If one thinks about it carefully, this seems to be a correct conclusion. One of laughter's most visible effects is to dissolve distinctions of all kinds.

Representations of the comic in Indian painting and sculpture occur much more frequently than is generally believed. This is because often they are secondary or complementary to images that fit the category of the erotic or amorous. Examples are to be found in the roly-poly dwarves so frequently seen under the feet or at the side of voluptuous goddesses and demi-goddesses (plates 13, 15 & 16). These fit the determinants of the comic listed in the *Vishnudharmottara*:

> Whatever is dwarf-like, hunch backed, or otherwise of deformed appearance...should be laugh exciting in sentiment.

Today such a statement would be considered politically incorrect in the extreme, but in practice it is not so very far from the world of circus clowns whose deformities are not repugnant and whose antics are not offensive.

A fine example of the comic grotesque is carved on the crossbeam of one of the gateways at Sanchi (plate 2). The work represents the temptation of the Buddha by Mara's demon armies just prior to his enlightenment. Although demons are generally associated with the furious and the terrible, these characteristics here are so exaggerated as to become caricatural.

In miniature paintings, specially those of the Pahari schools, there are many instances of the comic. Some of these hark back to the ancient tradition of naughtiness vis-à-vis the gods, albeit with considerable refinement and delicacy. Subjects like Krishna stealing the milkmaids' clothes and Shiva losing his loincloth (plate 24) exemplify this delightful genre.

In the latter part of the British period, when the freedom struggle was gathering momentum, several artists, most notably Gaganendranath Tagore, turned the comic into a weapon of protest in reproducible media like lithographs and woodcuts. In his trenchant caricatures and cartoon-like works, Tagore satirised not only the British but also the Indian elite who aped the colonials and danced, sometimes literally, to their tune (plate 25).

In post-Independence India, the satiric tradition has been carried forward mainly by newspaper cartoonists. But while many among these have been very gifted, none has produced a body of work comparable to the above. Again, the separation forced by our specialised times is responsible. On the one hand, there are satirists and humorists who are obliged for a living to fill column space on a daily or weekly basis and have, therefore, no opportunity to expand their artistic horizons. On the other hand, there are artists with every opportunity to evolve but who never seem to think that the comic flavour, now more than ever, needs to be revived in art.

One of the very few contemporary Indian artists to have found powerful expression in the satiric genre is Suraj Ghai (plate 26). Over the past decades, this artist has responded with trenchancy and wit to India's decadent socio-political fabric. In his drawings and prints he comments on the tyranny, hypocrisy and smugness of the ruling and middle classes through imaginative forms and economical lines.

Images of this kind are rarely forthcoming from artists of the 'liberal-left' who have aligned themselves with the struggle against fascism, religious extremism and economic imperialism. But these artists would do well to consider that they could be more effective if they were to remember that the comic is the artist's most powerful weapon.

The healthy attitude of the ancient Indians towards sex and the human body - above all, the female body - is reflected as much in the theory of *rasa* as in the art of the sacred monuments. In fact, every theorist or rhetorician who has ever written on the subject considers the erotic flavour supreme. *Shringara rasa*, as this flavour is known, is judged by all of them as *rasaraja* or *rasapati*, the king or lord of sentiments. When writing on the subject Coomaraswamy commented:

> What Chinese art achieved for landscape is (in India) accomplished for human love. Here, if never and nowhere else in the world, the Western Gates are opened wide.

Lee Siegel, who talks a great deal about *shringara rasa* in the context of the comic, prefers to translate this as 'the amorous' rather than 'the erotic'. In the sense that both pertain to sexual love there is nothing to choose between them. But the term amorous also means enamoured or being in love, as in the French *amoureux*; this brings it closer to the concept of *shringara* which, as emphasised by the theorists, arises from the enduring emotional state of love. Indeed, according to Vishvanatha, one of the most respected of *rasa* theorists, a courtesan cannot be a *nayika* or romantic heroine, through whom *shringara* arises, unless honestly enamoured. Of course, the term erotic once had an identical connotation; in Greek and Roman mythology, Eros and Amor or Cupid were as much concerned with women's and men's hearts as with their loins.

Bharata discusses *shringara rasa* in terms that contradict the image of sexual love that exists in the minds of most today. He says that the erotic flavour arises from:

> whatever is sacred, pure, placid and worth seeing...

It is also deemed the most exalted of *rasas* on account of its harmony with all aesthetic moods and enduring emotional states except disgust. Similarly, *shringara* is found compatible with all thirty-three complementary emotional states, excluding indolence and cruelty.

The word *shringara* is understood by most theorists to mean something through which a *shringa* is reached; a *shringa* literally means a horn or peak. But in the context of the erotic, as Goswamy suggests, it means

a peak or climax of delight.

Seen in this light, the tasting of *shringara* becomes a metaphoric orgasm, an explosion of ecstasy that penetrates and infuses the spirit.

At the same time, it must be reiterated that the experience of art and life are not the same. The spectator tastes the erotic without being sexually aroused by the hero or heroine or by the image or action represented. If this is what the spectator wants then seductive pin-ups or pornography are the answer. The purpose of art is not to titillate or arouse, but to refine the sensibilities, to heighten the senses, to improve the quality of life. Tasting the erotic flavour in art can and should enhance the sex life of the *rasika*, but it is not a substitute, it does not provide vicarious pleasure. The ancient Indians were well aware of this.

There are many who point out that there is a great deal of subjectivity in the question of art and obscenity or erotica and pornography. Some years ago, the editor of a 'girlie' magazine, was arrested for publishing allegedly 'obscene' pictures and a debate ensued in the national press. Needless to say this was inconclusive, since just about everybody - from would-be roué, Khushwant Singh to feminist, Madhu Kishwar - agreed that 'obscenity lies in the eye of the beholder'. Obviously none had heard of a science of aesthetics, Indian or other, which helps resolve the question.

Over the past few years there have also been several instances of reaction against nude images by right wing Hindu nationalist politicians. For absurdity, the most notable of these was the demand by some members of the ruling Bharatiya Janata Party for the withdrawal of a calendar published by the Delhi government on the grounds that a nude graced its cover. As a reminder of the facts, this was not just any nude; it was the little bronze figure called 'The Dancing Girl of Mohenjodaro', nearly five millennia old and a symbol of India's precocious civilisation. That those politicians found her obscene exemplifies the killjoy mentality - the culturally alien prudishness - of latter-day Hindu ideologues.

That such a mentality is hypocritical should be obvious, but the character and origins of sexual hypocrisy require a brief word. For this we can turn to the splendid Stendhal who observed when writing of Don Juan, the arch seducer and cruel breaker of hearts:

> For Don Juan to be possible, there must be hypocrisy in the world. Don Juan would have been an effect without a cause in Antiquity when religion was a celebration that exhorted men to pleasure... a large part of his pleasure consisted of defying opinion, and in his youth he imagined that he defied only hypocrisy.

The main truth to emerge from this is that those hypocrites who deny people pleasure do not merely prevent the liberation of society, they also encourage promiscuity and unleash perverts and criminals in our midst. All religions and ideologies, including those of the disparate Marxist parties, are now ruled by such hypocrisy, and the damage being done will take generations to repair.

Returning to the erotic flavour, many believe that in Indian art this means solely representations of couples in coitus. Nothing could be further from the truth. As Goswamy notes:

> it is the sentiment in all its subtlety of aspects, its infinitely variegated forms, that figures so prominently in the arts.

As far as the art of the sacred monuments is concerned, only a fraction of the works that fit *shringara rasa* are explicitly erotic, and most of these belong to a handful of temples of the medieval era. The remainder can be classified into two basic genres: firstly, images of loving couples known as *mithuna*, as opposed to copulating couples called *maithuna*; secondly, images of single female figures, generally goddesses and demi-goddesses.

These classifications are confirmed by theory; this states there are two kinds of *shringara*; love in union and love in separation. Miniature paintings of the Rajput, Mughal and Pahari schools follow the same tradition.

Both in Buddhist and Hindu monuments, images of loving couples in which the eroticism is implicit appear so frequently from the earliest times that they can be described as a leitmotif of Indian sacred art. They appear in a variety of poses, sometimes deeply relaxed, sometimes playful or even athletic, but always conveying an expression of togetherness, equilibrium and pleasure (plates 19 & 20). In the earlier monuments, these couples sometimes portray donors or patrons and sometimes demi-divinities with a foot in both worlds. In the later monuments they become the great deities, most often Shiva and Parvati.

The single female figure is no less a leitmotif of sacred monumental art but, unlike her counterpart in miniature paintings, she does not represent love in separation. She is a demi-divine or divine being in her own right. If she does have a consort, he is out the reckoning, out of sight. She does not yearn or pine for him. She is entirely self-possessed, cool and serene. Call her what you will: voluptuous, the essence of womanhood, the personification of sensuousness. But whatever one calls her she takes delight in her qualities.

Of course, not every female figure is finely executed; as with all art everywhere there are excellent, average and poor examples. In works of great excellence, her qualities are expressed in all their glory and she fills the spectator with pleasure. Much more than this, she makes the *rasika* taste the erotic; this is irrespective of the *rasika*'s gender.

In the Buddhist monuments, such figures are usually *yakshis* or tree nymphs. Among the finest of all is the *yakshi* who graces a bracket of the eastern gateway at Sanchi. One of the few extant examples of Indian sculpture in the round, she stands out for her supple, dancer-like pose, particularly apparent from the rear view (plate 13). Another wonderful *yakshi* is from a *stupa* at Mathura (plate 15) and like the former she belongs to the pre-classical period.

Among classical female figures arguably the greatest of all is the image of the Goddess Ganga at Ellora (plate 16). This humanised representation of India's greatest river is possibly an idealised portrait of a patron of the temple; her non-Aryan features suggest that she may be a queen of tribal origin. But whomever she might portray, she is majestic in her voluptuousness. No man could touch or approach her without her consent, and if he tried she would no doubt dispose of him with a flick of the wrist. The only classical figure to approximate her in sheer sensuality is that known as *The Dying Princess* at Ajanta (plate 27) but, as already noted, the predominant sentiment in that work is the pathetic not the erotic.

Returning for a moment to the Mathura *yakshi*, a blackening of her breasts and vulva may be noted, and this is evidently the result of her being touched by worshippers in antiquity. But on this account no-one should assume that these worshippers were all male. The *yakshis* originated in popular fertility cults, hence the purpose of their veneration was prosperity and propagation. Besides, as pointed out by Vidhya Dehejia, western feminist theories of spectatorship do not much apply to ancient India art. She says:

It appears that the gendered gaze may indeed function similarly in certain areas of secular art; however, in several other areas, it may not be too relevant.

She goes on to argue that the sensuousness of the female figure in sacred art had positive connotations for women. She cites evidence to support this when discussing patronage at Barhut, where voluptuous *yakshis* are much in evidence but where, according to inscriptions, over two thirds of donors were women, some of them nuns.

Dehejia further argues that the affiliation of woman with nature and fertility in Indian art has positive connotations because through this she becomes auspicious. She sees this as an explanation for:

the ubiquitous presence of woman on the monuments of India

and she cites ancient texts to confirm the correctness of this view.

However, a lapse appears in Dehejia's argument when she interprets the affinity between woman and tree. Discussing the ancient belief that a woman could cause a tree to bear fruit by her very touch, she states:

Woman's fertility was thus transferred, in a mysterious manner, to the tree; in turn, she too may have become more fertile through contact with its abundant foliage. The most popular legend concerned the *ashoka* tree...

One of the apparent reasons for her missing the wood for the trees is her unfamiliarity with Indian medical science. *Ashokarishtam* is a female tonic derived from the *ashoka* tree. It is widely prescribed to this day by Ayurvedic practitioners in order to promote fertility and the woman's general well being. It is therefore reasonable to infer that the women of ancient times nurtured the *ashoka* and other trees contributing to fertility and society's prosperity.

Nature otherwise has a place of paramount importance with respect to the erotic or amorous *rasa*. It is through nature that the lush and cheerful environment determining this flavour is created. This is confirmed by the determinants of *shringara* listed by Bharata:

> the pleasures of the season, the enjoyment of garlands, unguents, ornaments… playing and dallying.

Similarly, Vishvanatha lists the things that excite the erotic in the heroine and hero. These include:

> the moon, sandalwood ointment, humming of bees, an empty house, a secluded grove…

Such sensuous atmospherics are not only the creation of great dramatist-poets like Kalidas, they are abundantly visible in paintings and sculptures, including temple sculptures, of every era.

When listing the determinants of the erotic for painting and sculpture, the *Vishnudharmottara* speaks only of the basics of the human figure:

> That which shows beauty and nicety of delineation of form, and dress and ornaments according to the taste of the learned.

The *Vishnudharmottara* deals very cursorily with the theory of *rasa* in general. This is no doubt because the subject is dealt with so thoroughly in Bharata's magnum opus. Even colours are dealt with in detail in the *Natyashastra* and the section dealing with them is repeated verbatim in the *Vishnudharmottara*.

The only thing we learn from the latter is that in painting and sculpture the erotic or amorous had to be refined according to the tastes of cultivated people. And if we think about it today, this is still a valid guideline. Of all the areas of art, the erotic is much the most delicate and requires a very finely tuned mind to determine it.

One of the modern art writers who has contributed the most to our understanding of this issue is John Berger. In *Ways of Seeing*, his essay on the ways men see women, and women see themselves, triggered an international debate among feminist art scholars; thirty years on, the polemics continue. Indian art scholarship came into its own with the publication of the above cited volume, *Representing the Body: gender issues in Indian art*, edited by Vidya Dehejia.

When comparing erotic art in the European and non-European traditions, Berger makes some points of great relevance to our discussion on *shringara rasa*. He observes, for instance, that:

> Almost all post-Renaissance European sexual imagery is frontal either literally or metaphorically because the sexual protagonist is the spectator-owner looking at it.

The largest part of the imagery he refers to pertains, in fact, to female nudes the majority of which are painted in recumbent positions, as if awaiting the entry of the spectator. When talking of one such nude, a portrait of the actress Nell Gwynne, the favourite mistress of Charles II, Berger adds:

> It is worth noticing that in other non-European traditions in Indian art, Persian art, African art, Pre-Columbian art nakedness is never supine in this way. And if...the theme of a work is sexual attraction, it is likely to show active sexual love as between two people, the woman as active as the man, the actions of each absorbing the other.

156

Absorption is indeed the operative word when it comes to distinguishing the true erotic flavour in Indian art. In the case of a couple image - copulating or otherwise - it is mutual absorption. In the case of a single female figure, it is either self absorption - as in the case of a *yakshi* or goddess - or absorption in thoughts of the absent beloved. That the same logic can sometimes be applied to European art is suggested by Berger when he states:

> There are a few exceptional nudes in the European tradition... In each case the painter's personal vision of the particular woman he is painting is so strong that it makes no allowance for the spectator.

Surely the selfsame final words can be said not only about the nude or semi-nude goddesses of Indian art but about all images everywhere which reveal a woman's sensuality while safeguarding her dignity. She is not posing for the spectator.

At the same time one has to acknowledge that there are still some grey areas surrounding this issue. It therefore needs to be further explored by sensitive people from all walks of life. Towards this end, educationists might like to consider that art can be an invaluable tool in making the public aware of the difference between the erotic and the pornographic and in weaning people away from the obscene or titillating.

One way of achieving this is by introducing art images of nudes - male as well as female - in the classroom. In the initial stages this may cause sniggering and lewd remarks, but teachers will find that if they hold their ground and encourage discussions on such images, the silliness quickly passes. Art projected in this way becomes sex education's human face.

We would also do well to remember that there is a light and mirthful side to the erotic. As Lee Siegel asserts:

> Eros invests life with irony. Love is funny
> because it is so serious.

The erotic needs laughter and levity because sex and love-making are grave and profound in their implications and responsibilities. If this were not the case then human beings would not be distinguished from animals. The laughter of lovers is important precisely because it humanises sex. It bonds them as friends. It makes sensuousness fun.

That the erotic and the comic are compatible bedfellows was well understood in Indian tradition. In fact, according to the theory of *rasa* they need each other to survive. As already noted when talking of the comic *rasa*, figures conveying the erotic are often attended by comic or jolly figures. As to the theoreticians, while the later ones stressed that the comic could arise out of a mockery of any of the sentiments, Bharata understood comedy primarily as a burlesque of love. The *Natyashastra* says:

> The comic is a mimicry of the amorous.

Exasperated by the commotion brought about by confused lovers, Puck puts it simply in *A Midsummer Night's Dream*:

> Lord, what fools these mortals be!

In love, people become lunatic, childish, absurd; they say silly things, they act in a way that is funny to others. And when love is incongruous or unrequited the foolishness is heightened. Siegel explains where the line is drawn:

> The amorous sentiment manifests itself when
> the ideal is actualized; the comic sentiment
> manifests itself when the ideal is demolished.

Anil Karanjai's painting entitled *Egg Rise* (plate 22) exemplifies the amorous sentiment in a modern idiom. There are also elements of the comic in this weird, dreamlike image, which symbolises the creative energy released by sexual union. The absorption of the figures is self-focussed rather than mutual. And although one should not read too much in the work, one could say that through the figures' sublime detachment, the artist makes wry comment on the fleetingness of passion.

Men of the world think that pictures are made simply by moving the brush; they do not understand that painting is no easy matter . . . The artist must nourish in his heart gentleness and cheerfulness; his ideas must be quiet and harmonious.

Kuo Hsi
13th century Chinese artist

Can an image that yields the taste of the erotic - a deliberately sensuous image offer the *rasika* a taste of *shanta*, the quiescent, at the same time? And, as importantly, turning the question around, can an image in which the quiescent predominates also be sensual?

No, according to western tradition and theory. We have already seen that sensual imagery in European art was generally addressed to the male spectator, and it is axiomatic that its intention was hardly to fill him with quietude. Some of the 'exceptional nudes' John Berger talks of may reflect a serenity, but on the whole their intention is other than quietude: to reveal the intimate feelings of and for the beloved.

Modern western aesthetic theory also draws a line between the two. As Borev states:

> The less sensual and the more spiritual beauty is, the more sublime it is and vice versa: the more sensual, the more delightful.

Had Borev been familiar with Indian art, he would have changed or qualified this statement.

It would be an exaggeration to say that the more sensual an Indian image is, the more sublime or spiritual it is. But what can be asserted is that in Indian imagery where the erotic flavour predominates, there is a sublime or noble detachment from which emanates a feeling of serenity. It can further be said that in images of Hindu deities, or great men like the Buddha, which radiate stillness and calm, there coexists a sensuousness, subtle and sublime.

Obvious examples of the former imagery can be found in profusion at Khajuraho, Konarak and other medieval temple sites, as well as in miniature paintings of different periods and schools. In general, however, images of couples in coitus or at foreplay in temple sculptures project a greater quietude than the lovers in miniatures because miniature paintings so often illustrate a narrative which precludes stillness.

A much less obvious example is found in the Goddess Ganga (plate 16). Ganga's majestic sensuality has already been cited, but one also needs to focus on the tranquillity of the image. The figure is so stable, so poised, so tensionless as to become quietude personified or, more accurately, quietude deified.

And so it is in the finest images of the Buddha, like the head from Sarnath (plate 17) on display in New Delhi's National Museum. Representing the apogee of classical Gupta art, this work has become well known through replicas, yet most people miss its extraordinary qualities. For around five hundred years before it was created, artists had been striving to give concrete, human form to the abstract ideals illuminated by the Buddha in his philosophy of the Middle Path: equilibrium, the balance between extremes, and *nirvana* or infinite peace.

In the Sarnath Buddha the artist reached this goal. The image is at once abstract and representational, at once human and divine, at once unreal and realistic. Such a synthesis is special to Indian art. As Stella Kramrisch notes:

> The abstract and the realistic vision, which, as a rule, we hold apart as poles in the evolution of art, isolated by from one another by gradual

161

steps of development or by the sudden gap of reaction, are but the two sides of Indian art.

When one has tasted *shanta rasa* in contemplation of the idealised Buddha, one begins to ask the famous magical question: how did the artist do it? To answer this one has to look at the various elements that make up the image.

The first thing to notice is its geometric proportion and harmony. More than this, the whole head is composed of geometric elements: circles, ovals, straight and curving lines. The elongated ears are not merely a concession to the belief that such ears belong to the wise and that the Buddha was born with them. They are also an artistic device: if one tries in the mind's eye to shorten or otherwise alter the ears, then one sees the whole face losing balance. In fact, the ears serve to frame and give stability to the face.

Bringing the image into close focus, one sees much more than geometry: a heart shaped face with delicately chiselled features; the eyes formed like petals or fish; the brow arched like a great bird in flight. And what of the nose? To say that this looks like a meditating sage in lotus position may be a flight of fancy, but the head originally crowned a figure that would have been seated in just this position; imagination apart, the nose is essentially an abstraction giving depth and strength to the smoothly contoured, fleshy face.

It is in the Buddha's exquisite mouth that the image takes on its sensuous beauty. The gentle arches of the upper lips show a softness and delicacy; and with their fullness, generosity and tactility, the lower lips speak of a love for the goods things in life. This is a mouth most women would die for. And yet, it is beyond being touched.

None of this is to suggest that the creator of this masterpiece deliberately set out to portray a transcendental sybarite. As with every other part of the whole, the lips are designed to bring the desired qualities of equipoise, symmetry and substantiality to the face. One can see similar qualities in great images of Shiva, Vishnu or other deities. Ganga is again an example; though her sensuality speaks through the very form of her body, it is heightened by the ample, protruding mouth.

Even Leonardo's serenely detached figures, which come so close to Indian art, lack the sensuous tactile quality. Indeed, the synthesis was never achieved anywhere in the world except at sites like Ankor Wat which had their roots in Indian art. In India itself, an overall decline in patronage and aesthetic standards set in well before the establishment of Islamic rule. From around the 9th century on, only sporadically did sacred artworks reflect glimpses of their former glory. Much as one might admire medieval sites like those earlier cited, their splendour lies much more in their architectural concept and design; their erotic imagery is neither grandly sensuous nor sublimely tranquil like the imagery of the earlier Buddhist and Hindu monuments.

The achievement of the ancient Indian artists in many respects should never be underestimated. But this is specially the case with *shanta*, the quiescent *rasa*, for of all the feelings that can be communicated in an artwork, this is surely the most difficult to attain. And essentially it is only suited to the visual arts, music and poetry. But music and poetry are transient; the mood they create comes and is gone. Paintings and sculptures are a perpetual presence; this makes them the supreme vehicle of quiescence, of the mood of peace.

In Bharata's *Natyashastra* there is no *shanta rasa*. And later theorists who incorporated it into their canon stressed the difficulties of matching detachment with the aesthetic experience. However, it came to be agreed that since the *rasika* is not himself a great sage, he may taste *shanta* when it arises in art.

Influenced by Buddhism, some of the European modern artists, principally Paul Cézanne, set out to express the concept behind *shanta* through a new simplified language with nature as the vehicle. Cézanne wrote :

> We are a shimmering chaos. I come in front of my theme, I lose myself in it. Nature speaks to everyone. Alas, Landscape has never been painted. Man ought not to be present, but completely absorbed into the landscape. The great Buddhist invention, Nirvana, solace without passion, without anecdotes, colours!

It is often assumed that by following this path, Cézanne was escaping from the world's realities. In truth, this artist was a very conscious man and, as he makes clear, he chose to live in nature in order to evolve a visual language that speaks universally. The question then arises: why should a conscious man want to communicate a language that speaks of absorption in nature and release when the world is a sea of suffering?

Part of the answer lies with the Buddha. This radical reformist lived in one of the most violent epochs of Indian history and his actions and philosophy evolved accordingly. And so it was with Cézanne: he saw need to create order and stability out of the 'shimmering chaos', to bring this into balance and harmony. His philosophy too was that of a healer. But he never pretended to have reached his goal. More than anything else, he opened up a path. Picasso and the other Cubists took that path but soon deviated towards the urban. It was much later that the prophetic character of Cézanne's art became apparent.

A return to nature has marked the art and literature of every society in transition between one kind of rule and another. But never before our time have there been global mass movements not only to protect the natural and human environment, but also to rediscover the whole human being through reintegration in nature. Even in tiny urban spaces, often surrounded by squalor, people make efforts to live close to nature by creating gardens of pot plants and flowers. This can hardly be described as escapism. It is a way of coping with brute reality.

Art that has meaning serves this end, giving hope to people in their struggles to survive and change their condition. As Nietzsche put it:

> The great end of art is to strike the imagination with the power of a soul that refuses to admit defeat even in the midst of a collapsing world.

A similar end for art was defined by V. W. Van Gogh, nephew of the artist. Writing about his uncle in an exhibition catalogue he said:

> The appreciation of a work of art by the contemplator depends on its clarifying his own outlook, confirming or influencing his sentiments. What he wants is not to be afraid of the world he lives in; he does recognize its uncertainties but he does not want these to spoil his life. This attitude forms part of the struggle for existence which gives every individual a certain amount of dignity. This is what one finds in every great work of art... In Vincent's work there is the reflection of this human dignity. It is as if he wants his paintings to say: if our struggle is strong enough, we can see how marvellous our world is and what a fine place to live in it might be.

When art achieves this end, it soothes its viewers, leaving them with a feeling of greater equanimity and quietude. This has nothing to do with the subject. Strength, endurance, dignity and hope can be expressed in a human figure or face as much as in landscape; they can be expressed in a dilapidated hut, an empty chair or pair of old boots, in anything at all that strikes the imagination with directness and lucidity. They can also be expressed through any of the *rasas*, the odious and terrible included. Of course,

165

if *rasa* is missing the work will fail, for as continually stressed, it is *rasa* that brings a work to life and infuses it with feeling; it is *rasa* that carries the touch of art's original magic.

As an aesthetic system, a philosophical science, *rasa* can be described as a work of collective genius and one of India's gifts to the world. And like other of this country's great scientific systems, it needs to be revived and carried forward.

There is also a crying need to make more Indians aware of this magnificent intellectual and creative legacy. People cannot act on the present without knowledge of the past. They must understand their socio-political history, but it is as important for them to understand the history of their ideas and creative achievements. In one way it is more important: while socio-political histories point more to what could not be achieved, the history of art and science tells the story of a people's accomplishments.

But the history of art and science cannot be told in separation, as they have been until now. As long as art is viewed and taught as distinct from science, it will remain in the hands of experts and a tiny elite. This brings us back full circle to art's relationship with politics. Art is a political issue because people are cut off from the road that will lead them to understand it, a road also trodden by science.

Select Bibliography

A.L. Basham, *The Wonder That Was India*, Sidgwick & Jackson, 1954

Walter Benjamin, *The Work of Art in the Age of Mechanical Reproduction* appears in *Illuminations*, Fontana/Collins, 1973

John Berger, *Art and Revolution*, Writers and Readers Publishing Cooperative, 1969

John Berger, *The Success and Failure of Picasso*, Penguin, 1965

John Berger, *Ways of Seeing*, British Broadcasting Corporation and Penguin, 1972

Bertolt Brecht, *Brecht on Theatre: The Development of an Aesthetic*, first Indian edition, Radha Krishna, 1979

Yuri Borev, *Aesthetics: a Textbook*, Progress Publishers, Moscow, 1985

J. Bronowski, *The Common Sense of Science*, Harvard University Press, 1978

J. Bronowski, *The Ascent of Man*, British Broadcasting Corporation, 1973

Debiprasad Chattopadhyaya, *Science and Society in Ancient India*, Bagchi, Calcutta, 1979

Kenneth Clark, *The Romantic Rebellion*, Harper-Row, 1973

Vidya Dehejia, *Representing the Body: gender issues in Indian art*, Kali for Women, 1997

Ernst Fischer, *The Necessity of Art*, Penguin, 1963

S.K. Ghosh, *The Indian Big Bourgeoisie*, distributed by Subarnarekha, Calcutta, 1985

Lalitha Gopalan, *Coitus Interruptus and Love Story in Indian Cinema*, appears in *Representing the Body: gender issues in Indian art*, ed. Vidya Dehejia, Kali for Women, 1997

B.N. Goswamy, *Essence of Indian Art*, Asian Art Museum of San Francisco, 1986

Germaine Greer, *The Obstacle Race: the fortunes of women painters and their work*, Picador, 1979

Arnold Hauser, *The Philosophy of Art History*, appears in *Marxism and Art*, ed. Berel Lang and Forrest Williams, University of Colorado, 1972

Anil Karanjai, *Art Today*, Vol. 3, March 1982, ed. Jogen Chowdhury, Juliet Reynolds, Suvaprasanna

D.D. Kosambi, *The Culture and Civilisation of Ancient India*, 1964, Vikas Publishing House

Stella Kramrisch, introduction to and translation of The *Vishnudharmottara*, Calcutta, University, 1970

Richard Lannoy, *The Speaking Tree*, Oxford University Press, 1971

Lu Xun, *Waiting for a Genius*, Selected Writings, Volume 2, Foreign Languages Press, Beijing, 1982

N. Mukunda, *The Science of Beauty the Art of Thrill* was read at a seminar, *Aesthetics and Motivations in Art and Science*, Visva Bharati University, Shantiniketan, February 1993, published in The Statesman, October 10, 1993

George Orwell, *Charles Dickens (5) and Funny, But Not Vulgar, The Collected Essays, Journalism and Letters of George Orwell*, ed. Sonia Orwell and Ian Angus, 1968

Ozenfant, *Foundations of Modern Art*, Dover Publications, New York, 1952

S.A.A. Rizvi, *The Wonder That Was India (Volume II)* Sidgwick & Jackson, 1987

Amartya Sen, *Indian Cultural Manifestations and the West,* originally published in *The New Republic,* serialised by *Arts & Crafts* (New Delhi) between August & December, 1993

Lee Siegel, *Laughing Matters: Comic Tradition in India*, Motilal Banarsidass, 1989

Madanjeet Singh, *Ajanta*, Edita Lausanne, 1965

Theories of Modern Art, ed. Hershel B. Chipp, University of California Press, 1968, includes: the speeches of Adolf Hitler and George A. Dondero; *Manifesto: Towards a Free Revolutionary Art* by Leon Trotsky and André Breton; *Art and Politics* by Peter Selz

V.S. Wakanker and R.R.R.Brooks, *Stone Age Painting in India*, D.B. Taraporevala Sons & Co. Private Ltd., Bombay, 1976

Illustrations

On title page: *The Artist and the Connoisseur*, Pieter Breughel the Elder, pen and ink drawing , 1566-68, Albertina, Vienna

On Art and Politics title page: *Memorial to Builders*, Anil Karanjai, oil on canvas, 1979

On Art and Science title page: *Sketch of an Unborn Child*, Leonardo da Vinci (1452-1519), from his notebooks, Windsor Castle Library

Plates

1. *After You!*, Honoré Daumier, lithograph, 1868, Museum of Fine Arts, Boston (bequest of William P. Babcock)

2. *Mara's Assault* (detail), Sanchi, c. 1st century B.C.

3. *There is a lot to suck*, Francisco Goya, etching, 1799, Plate No.45 from *Los Caprichos*, Hispanic Society of America, New York

4. *Guernica* (detail), Pablo Picasso, oil on canvas, 1937, Guggenheim Museum, Bilbao

5. *The White General*, George Grosz, pen and ink drawing, 1919, collection of Erich Cohn, New York

6. *Bull's Head*, Pablo Picasso, bronze cast from bicycle saddle and handlebars, 1943

7. Head of a Nobleman, Mathura, c. 2nd century, National Museum, New Delhi

8. *David* (detail), Michelangelo, 1504, Accademia, Florence

9. *Dancing Wizards*, rock painting, Mesolithic Age, Bhimbetka, from a photograph by V.S. Wakankar and R.R.R. Brooks

10. Mimes or mummers disguised as animals, marginal illustration to the manuscript of *Li Roman d'Alexandre*, Flemish, c. 1340, Bodleian Library, Oxford

11. *Dukhopadana Jataka*, Suratghat, Mathura, c. lst century B.C., Government Museum, Mathura

12. *Starving Peasants*, Chittaprasad, linocut, early 1940's, courtesy Art Heritage, New Delhi

13. *Yakshi*, eastern gateway, Sanchi, c. 1st century B.C.

14. *Rishyashring, Gazelle-horned Ascetic*, Chaubara Tila, Mathura, c. 2nd century, Government Museum, Mathura

15. *Yakshi*, Bhutesvara, Mathura, c. 2nd century, Government Museum, Mathura

16. *The Goddess Ganga*, Ramesvara Cave, Ellora, late 5th - early 6th century

17. *The Buddha*, Sarnath, 5th century, National Museum, New Delhi

18. Sketch for *The Last Supper*, Leonardo da Vinci, c.1495, Musée Bonnat, Bayonne

19. *Mithuna*, Kondane, Cave 1, c. 1st century B.C.

20. *Mithuna*, Karle, c. mid-1st century

21. *Nymph and Rishyashring*, Kankali Tila, Mathura, c. 3rd century, Lucknow State Museum

22. *Egg Rise*, Anil Karanjai, oil on canvas, 1969, collection Juliet Reynolds Karanjai

23. *The Floating Conch,* Hieronymus Bosch (1450-1516), engraving by Pieter van der Heyden, 1562, after a lost drawing by Bosch, Rijksmuseum, Amsterdam

24. *Shiva's Snake Deserts Him*, Pahari, 1st quarter 19th century, Chandigarh Museum

25. *A Noble Man*, Gaganendranath Tagore, Chinese ink drawing, 1920s, courtesy Delhi Art Gallery

26. *Triumvirate of Evil*, Suraj Ghai, ink on paper, 1984, collection the artist

27. The Dying Princess, Ajanta, Cave 16, c. early 5th century, courtesy Madanjeet Singh

28. *Boddhisattva Padmapani* (detail), Ajanta, Cave 1, second half 6th century, courtesy Madanjeet Singh

Plates 2, 7, 11, 13, 14, 15, 16, 17, 19, 20 & 21 are published courtesy the American Institute of Indian Studies, Varanasi.